MOON OVEF
OWL IN
&
OTHER TALES
from
TURTLE ISLAND

by
Leona Graham-Elen
with
Family & Friends

THE BRIDESWELL PRESS

Dedicated to The One Work.

By the same author:
At Home in Bell Buckle
(Brideswell Press, 1995, ISBN 0-9649553-0-X)

Leona Graham Elen has asserted her right
to be identified as the author of this work.

First published 2002 in the United States of America
by The Brideswell Press,
PO Box 227, Topanga, CA 90290-0227, USA
info@brideswell.com http://www.brideswell.com/

Library of Congress Control Number: 2002090312

ISBN 0-9649553-1-8

Printed in Canada
by Hignell Book Printing, Winnipeg, Manitoba

Designed and typeset in Adobe Garamond
by Richard Elen at The Brideswell Press.

CONTENTS

Leona in Southern India at a Toda village, following the 6th World Wilderness Congress in Bangalore. The Toda are a very ancient, pastoral people. Photo by Vance Martin, The Wild Foundation, November 1998.

FOREWORDS

The Good Red Road into the Heart of Turtle Island

T HE 'STILL, SMALL VOICE WITHIN' has led me on an enchant-
ed, magical journey of a lifetime – out of Canadian acade-
mia, round the world, into the Findhorn Community in NE
Scotland, down through the Mists of Avalon in SW England – deep
into the Mysteries of the Matter of Britain. Then, back across the
Atlantic to the American South, where I stepped onto another
ancient Sacred Path, The Good Red Road into the Heart of Turtle
Island. My wee book, *At Home in Bell Buckle* (1996), covered a few
adventures on that path. In this follow-up work they continue, with
brilliant support from family and friends!

Whilst my partner Richard was always eager to develop his
American Dream in sunny Southern California, I'd vaguely avoided
it – a cautious Canadian approach. But by March 1996 we were On
The Road West, the '87 Blazer packed full, Bell Buckle belle of a kit-
ten perched between us. *Santa Monica, not Los Angeles*, was *my* goal,
enabling the fantasy that Santa Monica was *separate* from the
Fearsome Whole.

Occasionally I have allowed myself to like LA. Perchance I am
turning into an 'Angelina.' Mayhap only strong mystic souls can
resist, nay, transform, LA's paradoxical distractions, even from the
distance of Topanga Canyon's retreat, where we settled. And why so
many storytellers, in all their myriad disguises, are drawn here.
Hollywood must hold a deeper meaning!

When I began these poems, Richard and I were still married. The
gods of place seemed kindly disposed. And still, for months on end,
the sun may shine all day. Ravens, hawks and eagles do sky patrol.
Blue jays screech, dashing about on urgent bush business, driving
Caitlín the cat crazy. Humming birds dart to and fro. Peacocks
squawk and strut. Rattlers lurk. Dogs and coyotes howl. Ants, relent-
less. Chaparral and pine cover canyon walls. White and pink red ole-
anders proliferate. Lofty pepper trees droop wistfully, aromatic red
fruit mashing underfoot. Cacti sprout prickly pears. Grapefruit,
orange, lemon, apricot and plum trees blossom and fruit. Spiral stair-
cases wind up mountain sides; majestic peaks entice upward, beyond

lowland inland empires, smog-laden valleys and coastal dens. Topanga, sanctuary of natural delights, a hold-out, hints at what once was the golden paradise of The Red Queen Calafia: California.

Her sunny realm reveals hard truths, ones that may lie hidden in the mists of Avalon or latent in the South's lush gardens. Just as incessantly hungry Canyon critters devoured my attempts at gardening, so the gods of place tore away the fabric of our outer marriage, throwing us upon the mercy of other gods. And the 'inner voice' of the soul always opts for growth.

Following a righteous path requires listening, obeying, acting on guidance. Years ago, I wondered, when will Red Feather, Teacher on the Good Red Road, send the bill? Some sacrifice?

The answer came: Renewal. It didn't take much to get me back to Avalon in 1997 to support my pals with various Good Works, the Wise Crone Café and the Goddess Conference. Then Richard came, wanting divorce. True to my pattern of friendship first, we parted ways amicably. Despite trauma, free from marital imitations, my life transformed positively – from facing aging to saving wild cheetahs from extinction. Marriage bonds *and* binds. Renewing individual commitment to soul growth triggers transformation.

So The Magic truly began. A guardian spirit from the East, linked with my inner plane teacher, joined me. Next, the Angel of Findhorn – in league with Ojai's – whisked me back West to Ojai, California (45 minutes from Topanga on a good car day), to work for The WILD Foundation, the International Center for Earth Concerns and the 6th World Wilderness Congress (in Bangalore, India) and finally for the Cheetah Conservation Fund. Superlative opportunities to serve.

But the inner mystery of marriage demanded revelation. After all, Brigit, protector of brides and grooms, had blessed us thrice. We'd jumped her broom, been 'handfasted,' tied the good red cord. *This* relationship concerns The One Work, serving as 'helpmeets on the path'. And we'd met, been 'put together,' under magical circumstances, a convergence of Findhorn and Avalonian angels in a dragon castle on a super-natural Tor.

Brigit's healing powers were at work. Richard was ploughing through his mid-life crisis. The East called me back for family and friends. I packed my belongings and drove with my 87-year-old mother in the Blazer NE across the US, running Montana forest fires (getting my first US speeding ticket on my birthday under 100 miles from the Canadian border!). Visiting a niece married into the Ojibway Clan, above Lake Superior. Returning home to 'the other London' (Ontario, Canada). Then time in Florida supporting my sister Joan and her family, a perfect excuse to revisit Bell Buckle! Prior to Christmas 2000, a portal of opportunity for reunion with Richard opened up with a little help from my daughter. Brigit swept us through with her trusty broom! We drove our magic carpet (the Blazer) back across the country – via Bell Buckle! – dropping into places of power and possibilities. And here we are together again in Topanga.

The generous response to *At Home In Bell Buckle* has inspired me to venture forth from my cave to publish this work covering the years 1995-2001. The word *home* keeps surfacing! My journeying round the cardinal directions continually brings me home – where you, family, friends old and new and yet to come, live. *Home* is where the gods and angels place us, where nature spirits and perchance, elementals, accept us. Where the soul feels *at home*. To live and do The One Work (see *AfterWords*, folks!)

Believe in miracles, the mysteries, gods and goddesses, guides, angels, the greater good—and life will be filled with their magic— the poet reveals that *words* carry power; the mystic poet, that *living words* transform life.

With love from Leona
Topanga, California, USA, Winter Solstice, 2001

Family—Boyds, Grahams & Elens. *Outer pictures clockwise from top left:*
The Boyds (L-R) John & Nell (rear), Uncles Irving & Mac, and Aunt Thel;
The Grahams (1950s, London, Ontario); John Graham; Andrew & Alice Graham;
Kim, Leona & Florence; Margaret Elen, Richard & sister Frankie (August 2001);
Aunt Thel. Center: above, John & Mary Graham; below, Joan & Leona.
For Clan Graham genealogist Nellie Graham Lowry.

I: Coming Home in America
Back Home in Bell Buckle

That One Long Covered Dish Party
For Freeda Hall, remembered with love

It's easy to remember
That one long covered dish party
Since Life in the South still holds its magic well
A looking-glass world awaits the comer-in, invited guest,
And after all, I am an Alice-Mae[1] amongst other appellations

First we mingle in Her Lady's parlour
Stuffed with nostalgic treasures, mementos of bygone days
An array of flowery color, bright pink presiding, pale blue abiding
Ubiquitous patch quilts, button-down tables and footstools
Funky mirrors and fancy lamps, strangely erotic long-fingered
                                                    white china glove-hands

When all the dishes have appeared and the bucket of ice in place
We repair to the dining room backed up by the grand piano
And that one long covered dish party proceeds
Where it still goes on forever,
A-waiting this lost lady's return
To take her place beside the Queen of Hearts
To serve iced tea at thick oaken table
Heavy with Down South delights
Sticky sweet potato pie, ribs and chili to wonder at,
Potatoes every way and cauliflower too,
My Italianate salads merely passing muster
Acceptable new addition to old pioneer traditions
Unable to top the corn bread, barbecue chicken
And a host of old recipes dear to the Southern heart
'Cos dessert is yet to come...

1 I was christened well and proper, Thelma Alice-Mae... a name that could get
  me by in the South quite nicely.

Aphrodite
For Wanda

Sweet Goddess
Your ancient appellation may pass not through many modern lips
Yet You live on in bold eyes, buxom bosoms and swivelled hips
In the lilting messages of pagan country love,
Divine, mundane, eternally reborn unholy dove
Your siren songs of lust and loss draw down desires dear
Lyric verse or damned curse, your wand a spear

Magna Mater: Great Mother
For Linda Nannie, Bell Buckle Mayor

Magna Mater
Guarding her flock from cluttered aisles of antique pews[1],
Poet, trader, wife, weaver of bright colors and fine arts,
Mother to many, nanny to some,
Leading her rebellious flock through the hoop of a new time,
Untying the old buckle from the tree
Placing the venerable bell high up in some steeple,
How will it be in years to come when Bell Buckle
Bellows forth into the annals of Southern fame?
Will she be warmed by memories of feuds forgotten,
Fiends forgiven, friends foretelling future fantasies?
Mayor-mistress of this Tennessee Brigadoon[2]—
Where potters cast spells and poets mingle with old world magicians,
Artists hold the fayth[3] and songwriters slumber with ladies of peace,
Angels gay cavort along the strip where soldiers of fortune tell
long tales
To Southern belles who know the meaning of sacrifice.

1 Linda owns/runs at least one of Bell Buckle's several antique stores.
2 Brigadoon—that elusive, magical Scottish village that opens only once in a
  hundred years to outsiders, about which a wonderful movie was made.
3 Poetic license in honour of one of Bell Buckle's fine artists, Fay.

11

Singin' With the Sisters
On the Occasion of Visiting Bell Buckle at Thanksgiving Time
For Bell Buckle Bob

Late last night in the afterlight
Of a potent Bell Buckle Thanksgivin'
After Don's delightful pluckin'
And John's Blue Amazin' Grace
Bell Buckle Bob brought the sweet fandango
Out of our longin' souls by means of his truly gran pian-o
Whereupon did we sisters commence to sing
Our Wisdom Circle made round agin,
Come-back supremes in gospel harmony
Lead by the Divine Firenze, Queen Anne and First Lady Liz
With goodly Sir Buzz bringin' up the bass
And yours truly on backup
At home again in a Deep South that never was but in the
                                        bright imagination
Of so many souls bent on sweet salvation
That a church at every corner
Can barely contain the pride and loss and pain

Soldier of Fortune
For Mr Crabtree, Bell Buckle Vet

You keep the watch
Whilst we rest
Make lackadaisical livings

In this town where time plays tricks
With the co-operation of a community
Practising the presence of joy

Timekeeper, walking through ages,
Accounting for battles won or lost
By an uncanny code, reckoning cost

We, your captive wedding guests, brimful of wonder,
Etched against the haze of summer days
And the mixed metaphor of a Middle Tennessee winter

You say the black captain has been taken
As you watch from your timepiece in the stars,
A satellite from out a future yet to unfold

You speak of dangerous liaisons in Atlanta,
Or the count of royalty in lands far to the north
As you piece together the meaning of us all

You walk the strip of Bell Buckle's present
But the past swirls round you as you pass us by,
Casting revelations with your uncanny divinatory art

Some ancient spirit holds you captive.
At his absolute and express command
You must pass his messages to us mere mortals

Like the Ancient Mariner to the Wedding Guest.
But why this albatross and what seas
Did you both wander, what ladies left untouched?

This is my tribute to your wayward fortunes,
A man lost and found in times of war
Your sweetness shining through your crabapple bark.

A Thrill Down Blueberry Hill
For Anita

Sprite from realm of faerie,
Pixie casting magic spell,
Woman wrapt in her peculiar hell
Fate tricked this south'n gal

All she ever wanted was
A thrill down Blueberry Hill

Girls grow up, dreams die down,
Pain comes long to stay
No matter what won't go way
Still she gives us her time of day

A fence the wind flattened
A roof rain rendered holy
She fixes, but there's no magic moly
To cure her crazy melancholy.

'Cos still she craves
A thrill down Blueberry Hill

She bears the censure
Sling shots and dirty darts
By Bell Buckle's better parts,
Despite her friend the queen of hearts

Bell Buckle's bestest buffalo gal

Footnotes for the poem opposite:
1 Alexander Graham
2 Ian=John=Sean, versions of 'the first son' and in our case, great grandfather
  John Graham who brought our line to Canada, named after his father, and the
  name of my eldest brother's first son.
3 A natural math genius, he became an assessor, master-measurer, a teacher of
  assessors. In ancient times, these were our sacred geometers, designers of cathe-
  drals, pyramids and landscape temples.

Brothers Three

For my three blood brothers,
Bob, Ralph (pictured with Leona in 1954) and Ian Graham

Both younger brothers drive pickups
Like guys do here in Tennessee
Ralph's got a beat-up old black one
With room enough to sleep a wee boy
Driving south to Florida to fulfil doomed dreams of family,
Passing me by way of meeting Highway 75,
Our Daddy's namesake[1] tumbling out of a boy's sleep
                              into a man's land,
Where pickups may measure commitment
                        to the American Dream
Going ever West, living out On The Road,
Where cattle, horses, dogs, dead deer, expired coyotes
And other savory road-kill roll before their final destinations
In slaughterhouse deep freeze or a sorry grave
unworthy of the gravity of death

My friend Rosanna tenderly picked up
a dead barn owl
some pickup man drove over
Saving the feathers to honor the dead,
she buried the body on holy ground

There's Ian, live coyote brother, last son named for first[2]
Searching with Red Feather Masters for truth of truths.
He may succeed where others fail, finding God's trail,
Traveling to Old Lands of lost gods
Our forebears carried with them
Across a new world in covered wagons
His Fire-Red Chevy truck, a mixed metaphor in memory
Of first sons on weary steppes.
Our destinies meet mirror-wise: before he was a pickup man
We met by no chance on the Trans Canada Highway going west
Driving with my ex and a sleepy, tousle-headed baby girl
In our painted Volkswagen van,

When the music of the 60's inspired us
With visions of better worlds, before John died,
I cried "It's my brother!"
We picked him up, he'd just climbed up from the gully,
                              having braved a bear
There's something about a pickup that takes us back in time

But Bob, first son, made in his father's image,
A navy man who would go one further and fly fast planes,
He faced his demons at the bottom of the bottle
After following our father down that slippery slope.
But he never drove a pickup, passed them by in biker days,
Nearly died, no easy rider, lived to teach the measure of matter.[3]
Eldest counsels younger, younger loves youngest,
Youngest Walks Far.
Will their pickup days pass, will they fly moon-wise
As Dad would have done if he could?

Meanwhile, we sisters busy ourselves in matters of the heart,
Aligning the culture of head
To the serious disposition of the soul.
Joan has abandoned the culture of the car,
Claiming cities for people, streets for feet…
Whilst I reluctantly pick up the Chevy Blazer registration
                              from the bureaucratic maze
As we prepare to make our way westward
Across the Heartland of America

Dust[1]

By my partner Richard
(pictured at a stone circle in Cornwall)

Along the flowered highway[2]
Stands an ancient farmhouse gray,
Where Richard and Leona
Spend many a joyful day

If you look inside a room you'll see
That all is spick and span:
The floors are scrubbed;
The beds are neat;
And everything's in hand.

But look a little closer, yet
And you can plainly see,
While Leona's space is clean and bright
It's Richard's that can't be.

Dust, dust
He hates dust
It makes him sneeze,
It makes him cough,
Just a little is enough
To make him swear
To make him cuss,
'Cos he hates dust.

Peruse Leona's bedside
And you'll be pleased to see,
That every shining surface
Is clean as clean can be
But over on the other side,
Lie cobwebs, dirt and rust
Because that side is Richard's side
And he hates dust.

Dust, dust etc

And when the sunlight streaming in
Reveals it, you can see
The shining motes of dust that float
Around the old debris
And when upon a morningtide
The daily sheet is shook
The motes all land on Richard's stuff
And never on her book.

Dust, dust etc

There's dust above
And dust below
In every single space
He says "It's just an accent"
And "Please leave it in its place"
"If I don't bother it," quoth he,
"Then it won't bother me,"
But Leona knows
That it just grows
Around him ceaselessly.

Dust, dust, etc

The dust is in the carpets
It's on the rugs and tiles
It hangs around in cobwebs
On tables and in piles

There can be no solution
To this problem, ages old
Though to the dust there's seldom been
A poem like this told.
Some folk seem to collect it,
While others clear away,
And me? Well, I'll just leave it,
For another day.

BACK HOME IN BELL BUCKLE

Dust, dust
I hate dust
It makes me sneeze,
It makes me cough,
Just a little is enough
To make me swear
To make me cuss,
'Cos I hate dust.

1 This poem, written *en route* from our home in Bell Buckle, TN, to see some
   friends in North Carolina, was inspired by the meter of J. R. R. Tolkien's 'The
   Mewlips' from *The Adventures of Tom Bombadil*, as is evident from the very
   beginning, and lines like "The shining motes/of dust that float", that have a
   kind of quasi-Anglo-Saxon short line/long line feel to them (believe that, and
   you'll believe anything...).
2 A reference to the part of Highway 82, (a main road through Bell Buckle)
   between the town and Highway 231, which was planted with daffodils,
   allegedly, by students of Sawney Webb (a relative of the Malibu Webb) who
   founded Bell Buckle School. You can read more of the story on page 44 of *At
   Home In Bell Buckle.*
PS: *Somehow, the dust seems to have followed me to Topanga... —Richard*

On the Road West with Caitlín, our Bell Buckle cat, on her very long leash...

Dealing in the American Dream

Dream of Turtle Island
For Vance

We pass through Arkansas, Little Rock up ahead
Where so much happened not so very long ago[1]
When Rosa Parks sat in on an ordinary bus
In an extraordinarily simple act of courage[2]
Bringing A Dream alive for others to step up into
At every bus stop in America

This is the Dream of Turtle Island
This ranging free and high riding west
Where visions come true
When we pursue them from soul level
Where spirit has room to breathe
This is not to say that the journey is easy, the way made clear

We cross the Mississippi, Grandmother of Rivers
The plains encompass us
Red Feather's rattle and drum, medicine wheel, red and white
Turn our thoughts towards the Hoop of Creation
For once, too long ago to count
We crawled up from under the earth
Through the hole of the Mother
To greet the Sun and know ourselves For The First Time

We are always coming home in America
The Old Ones greet thirsty newcomers
Encircle us with the golden light of providence
Pass us through the Hoop of Hope
Bend us to the Will of Manitou
We may dance round fires
Eat salmon of wisdom from wild rivers
Coyote wolf bear watching from afar,
Celtic Shawnee bloodlines merging, remembering us.

We are, we are not, welcome in this land of plenty
We pass initiations into the Clans of Turtle Island
We turn around inside ourselves to know this place
Once again as Home

1 Remembering September, 1957, when nine African-American students chal-
  lenged white supremacy at the Central High School
2 In Montgomery, Alabama, in 1955

After Abilene

After Abilene we drove west again,
Having negotiated the dangers of Dallas
Slick roads and sirens,
A maelstrom of truckers trapped on the 635W
Debating on CB how to get the fuck off
Whilst we watched 635E grind to a halt, confirming
The gridlock theory of American carma

A Red Carpet Inn laid out its seedy magic
Meeting place for aging wheeler dealers and busty broads,
But the cable was good so the Weather Channel
Replayed the day's hazards, green and orange blobs
Spiraling down the storm's ragged corridor
From Battle something to Durant, like the scanner said,
Whilst in between there was the reality of it all
Scary green tornado skies to the right
Rolling black clouds to the left, though off to the west
There was a white sun

Texas roads run long, straight and dusty,
Leading somewhere for some reason, alongside
Old shacks, abandoned gas stations, sagging corrals,
And little monster oil pumps dragging up the remains
Of a carboniferous Eden we squander
In contemporary covered wagons and metallic carpets
NASA cowboys ringing the stars for our pleasure

The smell of crude oil fills the mind
With life-threatening scenarios
Even a grand slam breakfast cannot dissolve
If this mean, dispirited landscape funds the good life
We have hell to pay
The end may buy a condominium on the Florida Keys
Due to flood annually till Atlantis comes again
But in between is the nightmare of the cost
Tattered down'n'outers at bummed-out cafés
This unrighteous human condition
Where too many suffer to send a few to heaven's gates
Where millions starve so some can die obese
This Grand Chasm in the American Landscape,
This too, Turtle Island's inheritance,
As she grinds across the continental plates
Seas swinging round her
We can only hope her destination
Includes our descendents, her destiny our dreams.

The Brotherhood of Truckers

On the occasion of driving
from Tennessee to California 1996

All the way across America
The brotherhood of truckers tracks the Soul of the Land
In Arizona accents sweet and southern
Mix with harsher northern tones
The democratic Citizen's Band broadcasts stories
About A People At Work
Weather advisories, journeys' ends, hoped for destinations,
Warnings of smoky bears and alligators
Available at no cost to alien roadrunners,

Us truckie wannabes and them celluloid businessmen.
They discuss dust storms, how Arizona can blow away
Into New Mexico one day
Over into Texas the next, and then back again in a few days
Sharing dirt, seeds, Mother Earth's eco-librium.
Just now we were called a little four-wheeler
Likely nearly served up for lunch 'less we got out of the way.
They know we've got our ears on,
Best behave or we're for breakfast.
All considering, not too much fuck-this-an-that,
There's ladies on board,
Lighter, warmer tones mellow up against (ho hum) real men's.
At the last stop a beautiful boy with blond hair down to his waist
Shared coffee and hash browns with hardcore lifers,
Expansive with trucker food and timed travel.
They see America across a broad spectrum
Through a wide lens, an endless elongated road ahead,
        path reasonably clear, paycheck waiting wives and needy kids
Philosophers of the road, grounded geographers,
Dealers in multi-perspectives, vertical line against horizontal
Sacred geometry super natural watching suns rise and set
                                moons pass over stars.
The Big Chill lies in the jackknife, lines jar, straight goes crooked,
                                heads up heavenward
Where the greatest trucker of all
Sits in His Dad's Divine Diner
Drinking His last cup at the counter
Before returning to The Road
But always ready to stop awhile and chew the fat.

Come On!

Coming Home In America
For my niece Laura and her partner Verne

We are always coming home in America
                              —so say the Hopi, our Elder Brothers
We went astray, wandering high steppes, along dark rivers,
Lowlands by silver seas, over oceans, crossing continents,
Discovering, as if for the first time, exploring, returning
We had forgotten all we were.
From East to West we trekked across the vast back of Turtle Island
Casting covetous eyes upon the naked beauty
Of a Western Queen the Spanish called Calafia,
Her golden body glittering under a bright, Otherworldly sun
Where once 300,000 acolytes thrived
                              in gardens of delight by azure seas
It has been a long journey homeward
                    wherein we have not yet remembered ourselves
                    nor recalled the image in which we were made,
Preferring a Roman symbol of perfidy
To the Hoop of Hope, to gratitude and grace of giving.
We have made of homecoming a hard endeavour.
We refuse to recognize who we displaced and why.
We are a stubborn people full of wrath from an eastern god
Not ours in our beginning, taken from an unwilling people.
Now in the modern mirrors of psychotherapy
Those who try to scry the natural shape of things,
                                        confused and weary,
Counsel the rest, refuged under clouds of unknowing,
                              having replaced gods with gold
Sliding by shadows of selves we could be for our children's sake
It has been a long journey and we will have not arrived
Until the last First American and we are won.

California Dreaming
On Coming to California in March 1996
For Colleen (inset), in anticipation of your first visit

We dropped down from the high hills
Through the pass on Interstate 10, clear across from Texas
The sun had just set, skies streaking peach blue
City lights competing with emerging stars
Palm trees stark against darkening light, potent atmosphere patent
Nostalgic strains of *Yellow Submarine, Magical Mystery Tour*
Resounding across landscapes of memory
      For him, Hawaiian Tropic in an old VW
      For her, Haight Ashbury's mixed ecstasies
Propelled to Palm Springs, Ky-Toya, healing waters of the Cahuilla[1]
The Estrella welcomed us in, bougainvilla blooming,
                        strong citrus scents,

Hot azure pools invited play,
            sly glances from a grey generation.
The Angel of California had kept a place for us
            these twenty-odd years and more
She dreamed us and we her

She will have us for lunch

1 The native people of that region

Santa Monica Mountains—seen from Topanga

Shifting Sands and Noble Precipice
For Ishi [1]

Life on the Southern California freeway – an abiding desire to negoti-
ate successfully at any cost, hoping like hell to get away with it, hang
out, enjoy it long enough in the sun by the sea near the mountains
before death, despair, depression, debility or mere discovery damn you –
throw in a dram of eco awareness and liberal thinking, maybe not,
they come and go in the ephemeral domain of storytellers, impressarios,
mesmerists; earthquakes, fires, mudslides, high costs, crowding, night-
mare windshield, drive-by and school shootings, gun as god, gang wars,
drugs...

Soon, from beneath the soil, shifting sands, noble precipice
                                        and hidden cave
Broken bones of old shamans heal, re-membering,
Battling new gods whose strategy of denial falls before them,
Shame seeps in, purifying the Soul of the Land, her People,
Green Corn Gods rise as the Rainbow Dolphin Tribes return,
Renewing ancient contracts with Turtle Island
 – the modern appellation, 'America'[2] dropping away, a passing
                                whimsy, happenstance honour.

Alive, the canyons, deserts and holy woods again resound
with calls to a new resistance to injustice, rape, murder, racism, sex-
ism, genocide, misogyny, planetary pollution, ruthless new robbers
called pioneers and developers, those who made Ishi the last of his
line, meeting their match in the new pacification of the Pacific
Rim.

For even as they drank themselves dumb, screwed up and reinvigorated
the mystery of the world gene pool, the dolphin secret arose, that all
living things are linked in one vast chain of being, in harmony with
all other realms of existence, beyond the desire for territory to bear
children, the memory of lost lands and endless treks, down from the
Altaic Homeland[3] in the Russian Steppes, across the wide plains of
Poland, along the dark rivers of middle Europe, out of Rome with the
barbarians, back through Constantinople to enchant the East,

*remembering the secret of Tarquinia in the land of the Etruscans, the
white light of Apollo's Greece, Mercury's transformation into Celtic
Lugh⁴, moving ever westward, from Rome, to Gaul, to Merlin's
Enclosure – Brigit's Britannia, Banba's ⁵ Eire, Islands of High Desire,
not forgetting the Celtic homelands South to Iberia from whence new
barbarian hordes with the cross of their Eastern saint made haste to old
lands called new worlds*

Their lost kin awaited them in this ancient new land, no guns, no horses,
Greeted them ashore, as in time the serpent turns tail to meet itself.
So shall we not take a stand here on shifting sands and noble precipice
To be one with the old gods who planted this paradise?

1 Ishi, the last Yahi Indian (California tribe).
2 German clergy-scholar Waldseemuller named the 'new found' southern conti-
  nent (S America) after the 'inconsequential' 15th Century Italian explorer
  Amerigo Vespucci in honor of his 'discovery' of the new 4th portion of the
  world. He changed his mind later, but too late as his 'Carta Mariana' was used
  in Gerardus Mercator's 1538 definitive world map, showing S and N
  'America.'
3 When this was originally written, perhaps; the current view is that the Indo-Europeans, and thus the Celts, derive their common ancestry from Anatolia, in what is now Turkey.
4 Celtic God of Light
5 According to John and Caitlín Matthews, the first settler of Ireland, called "The Island of Banba of the women," or *Tir na mBan*, is one of the three goddesses of Sovereignty.

Joshua Tree National Park, CA

Drunk On America

For the late Tom Buchan, Scots poet, lover, friend
on the Occasion of the Democratic National Convention 1996

Tom didn't like America
But I dedicate this poem to him,
Hoping he hears high in the heavens he doubted
He hated the brashness, imperial thrust, jingoistic verbiage,
Attitudes British once were blamed for
But I have fallen in love with America

Ah, Tom, if only you could have seen
The proud Mexican American from Texas
The happy Philippine governor from Hawaii
The native American with his drum
Behind the speaker from Nebraska
The glow of the black Mayor of Detroit.
No, this is not to say they will not fall from grace

You might wonder
At the destiny of this joy and despair drunk land
Filled with the ecstasy of desire, a magnificence of hope
Even the President hails from a town called Hope[1]
Though Little Rock is his just domain,
The New South reclaimed
The visionary Vice-President waiting his turn in vain[2]

If only you could have been beside us, Tom,
As we toasted the American Process,
However bitter the betrayals, the cost, the glitz…
These are the descendants, sent westward,
Of the dispossessed, deprived, sent down from the Highlands,
Satanic English mills, Welsh mines
From Clearances and Famine
Survivors from Eastern Europe
Mexicans come to take back what they lost

Drunk on America
I sing the song that Walt [3] sang
Know now what he knew

1 Then-President Bill Clinton.   2 Then-Vice-President Al Gore.   3 Whitman, not Disney.

28

Mad Car Disease

For my sister Joan, radical green cyclist

Cars and houses
Litter the doorway to the soul's desire
Block up free spirits
In prisons perfect without bars

Doom the dreamer
Mess up the mind
Vanquish the victor

Cars

Making them manifesting them maintaining them
And then selling them salvaging them sacrificing for them
Driving them depending on them dying in them

and

Cars extend feet
And arms but
Render us immobile

Damning us in traffic queues
Insinuating themselves
        into serious conversations
Severing us from real life
Erecting false ego values
Annoying us at every turn
Separating us from good sense
Ensuring life with debt

Houses

Cage the soul
And strangle the spirit
Garrotte free will
Execute mortgages on good

*Joan with her bike
at a protest rally.*

        and bad alike by the guillotine of household finance

together they compr(om)ise

Shelter	Society
And	As we know it
Navigate us	Navigates
Intransigent	Its
Transient	Truth upon their
Yahoos	Yoke

PS: This poem could have gone on forever. It's just stopped for the time being...

Messages From Earthly Space
For Ann H (right) & her daughters
Robin (left) and Kim (center) pictured opposite

27 to 101 Southeast to the San Diego Freeway,
405 to Interstate 5 to La Jolla, 2½ hours of rippling cement,
       earthquake retrofits, several near misses, gray outlooks,
Tantalizing scent of sea air, multiple lookalike turnoffs
To multiple lookalike gas stations and multiple lookalike fast
       food joints
Passing multiple images of myself in other SUVs
Listening to *The Wave*, hoping for the best, the worst
Will pass, will I ever arrive at a destination I desire?

We advance to Encinitas
Where Yogananda joined West to East
At the command of his lion king Yukteswar[1]
This is neither hell nor heaven nor simply middle earth
Is this what limbo is, this mix of New Age wash, Hindu linen
The chinking sound of cash machines with muzak motivators,
Barbara Sher's handy radio truths for hungry souls?
What once was difficult is now distortedly accessible,
       what secret, now for sale
Or am I merely mean-minded, miserly, mistaken?
After all, in America everything can be bought or sold,
To have, to hold, is this not freedom?

Good guides lead us past such phantoms of this foretold time.
We listen harder, pray more silently, watch most carefully.
When windows open of themselves and light comes too,
The scent of roses and lilacs sent by angels to us undo,
And touch, taste, the substance of love when it flies through,
So then my sisters, we need not wonder at the way
It was inside that chapel by the sea
How dolphins passed us by and whales spouted high in hope
We would take their tale back to our unkind and change the world,
How that special seal lifted her shiny head
From the silvery sea and spoke a language deeper
Than our tongues can navigate, to tell you little sisters
What it is we need to do, to save her selves to save the sea
To save the world, it's all part of each generation's key.
Watch that lame and bright beady-eyed bird use his will
To get his way with us at lunch
All these are messages from earthly space,
We need not go so far to listen in.

1 Sri Yukteswar: the guru of famous Indian teacher Paramahansa Yogananda,
   founder of the Self Realization Fellowship.

Mr Toad Goes to Hollywood[1]

We met high on a hill in Avalon's holy land[2]
Where golden apples grow and scrumpy[3] grabs the knees
Found a hobbit house way from the madding crowd
Of Merlins and Morgans and minions many,
Baked green pie in the sky and fought the Iron Lady[4]
Curled up against the damp of Britain's unblest clime
Married thrice for luck, once up against the law,
We jumped her broom, he were her stag,
Brigit[5] blessed them both, be sure of that

But from cross the seas a Siren Song came calling
A peradventure for a Prince who found the English galling
So we trundled off to Tennessee—the new country
Where Cherokee were cheated and Creek were drowned
But still the Siren sang like a true *amie* [6]
Be she Calafia or some other enchantress queen
Turn'd Prince to Toad who'd come to Hollywood
To meet his match
So Lady Frog might turn herself to some other nobler catch.

1 Since writing about our separation,
   we have come together again.
2 The Tor, considered a gateway into
   the Celtic Under/Other World.
3 A potent West Country English hard
   cider that can make knees crumple!
4 Served in the Green Party; dealt with
   life under PM Margaret Thatcher.
5 The Fire Goddess Brigit protects
   brides; may explain our re-union.
6 Play on the word 'anima': Jungian
   term for a man's bewitching signifi-
   cant inner female 'other.'

Leona and Kim-Ellen at LA County
Courthouse after doing the Response to
the Petition of Divorce

Neruda
On having seen the film Il Postino
For Elizabeth and Graeme Bieman

We need people poets like Neruda,
Large, full, overflowing, in love with life,
Thinkers who dare, lovers who care
Things are better when we commit ourselves.

Anna Maria, my Chilean sister,
Savagely cut away her long black river of hair
When a Free Chile died with Allende, exiled in Canada,
Her way to say, this my beauty I give for my dream destroyed

We need the poet who stands tall,
Words telling guns where to go,
Remembering us to our ancestors,
Druid princes who chose sacrifice, queens like Boadicea

A poet's words even in translation
Can gush into the soul, surprise from within,
Resistance to truth falters, transforms to courage
In a world run by images of what to buy, why and how

Such a poet's letters arrive with hopeful alternatives

Words bring us alive
Phrases feed us
Lines rebuild us
Stanzas stand up

For epic endeavour

Walking With Charlie
*On the Occasion of Taking a Walk
with Charlie Cooke, Chumash Chief*

I awoke, clear message in mind,
Called by a Chumash Spirit
To Satwiwa, bluffs behind suburban sprawl

Charlie tapped the Inner Telegraph
Inviting us to walk his people's holy hills
We went, were welcomed, will come again

We did not miss his blessing, smoke that purifies—
We had it in the night, when dreams call
Wayward wanderers home to medicine wheels

Feather in his red cap, was this
Red-Feather Man over seeing our return
To the Good Red Road which runs within the soul
His staff of eagle there before us
Lady ranger taking up the rear
We walked his talk regarding matters of the land

Root of tula, flower from yucca, chia seed in sage,
Willow bark, black walnut, long and live oak
Soapweed, sumac, mugwort and miner's lettuce

A red winged black-bird flew ahead
Coyote droppings marked the trail
A sparrow hawk circled high above

Charlie told his tales as tourist
Hikers passed us by, missing his points
We turtle-islanders will seize that day
A motley little tribe of twelve or more
We were ready for revelation
Slowing down we turned around

And saw what too few see
The life in little matters
Meaning within the heart of things

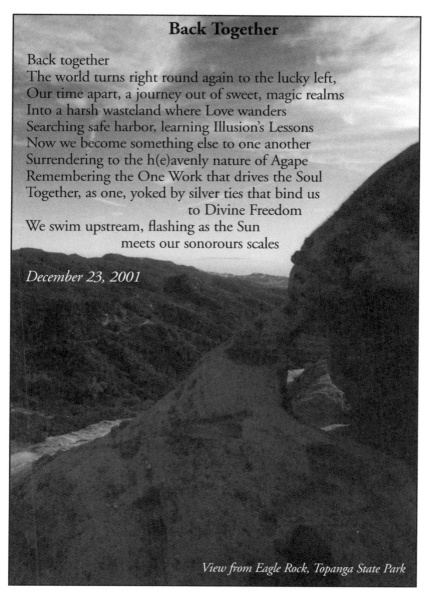

Back Together

Back together
The world turns right round again to the lucky left,
Our time apart, a journey out of sweet, magic realms
Into a harsh wasteland where Love wanders
Searching safe harbor, learning Illusion's Lessons
Now we become something else to one another
Surrendering to the h(e)avenly nature of Agape
Remembering the One Work that drives the Soul
Together, as one, yoked by silver ties that bind us
                    to Divine Freedom
We swim upstream, flashing as the Sun
                    meets our sonorours scales

December 23, 2001

View from Eagle Rock, Topanga State Park

II:
NORTH EAST PASSAGES
&
OLD WORLD INTERLUDES

The
best hex
(of all)
is knowing
what's best
for oneself at any given time
in relationship to what's best
for everyone else
(and the planet of course)
with this knowledge a woman is supreme
in touch with the Cosmic Hex
The Creatrix
We can put aside all the other little scams and trickeries
Lies and spies and meaningless ties
Knots and crosses, athames
and statuettes that bleed
Our long tall cone
of a hat and pointy nose
So there we are,
witches
who
were

The Best Hex (of all)
For Sue Boone, on the Occasion of the Founding of
our London Agape Group, January 2001

Canada

Full Moon
By my daughter, Kim-Ellen

full moon
beams
criss cross
the night

spoon fulls
of
moon beams
dance
like sugar drops
on tarmac
criss crossed
the iced

cocktail
night
at Diana's
disposal
shed
clouds
and
high winds
earth changes
position
dear
Goddess
Shine your light on me

Bellatrix-O Lion
By my eldest brother, Robert (pictured)

Raised to hunt or gather?
Mark the 'Word'
        The sender 'Fourth'
Not Momism- Big Brother
        Phantoms in the Night of Time
You Are Alive
        This Is To-Day
                Forever!
God the Father
        Not All the Sons and Daughters
One and Only One
        First and Last
                And Forever!
Rise From the Flesh
        And Be!

Become A Plus
        Then You Can Enter Forever!
The Body Is the Test
Have You Been Tried?
        Or Are We Playing Games?

Love – Brother Robert
        To Sister Alice-Mae

Late Pregnancy
By my friend, Elizabeth Bieman

To grow old is to be pushed to the side of your own life.
— Christopher Ricks on Philip Larkin's "Afternoons" in *The Force of Poetry* (Oxford 1984)

Ricks, on reading Larkin, cautions me:
something is pushing me off to the side
of my own life.
True that was, in Larkin,
of the lives of his young afternoon mothers.

I remember.
I rarely could find time to find myself
in any way as I gave way perforce
to "somethings" I had borne, "somethings" I loved.

Larkin spoke afternoon truth from observation.
Ricks is merely wrong –
because he speaks too soon and as a man
his general observation will not hold.

This crone has known the years of Larkin's mothers,
the self expanding, centre pushed to side.
But now in age the self comes, blessed, back
to centre –almost full, "thickened" in Larkin's word
by life – till life shall pass.

Copyright ©2001, Elizabeth Bieman

For An Aikido Teacher
By my friend, Penn Kemp

A ghost
    floats   through my class
as students crowd their mats:

              "What is Maai is not yours."

Who am I to him, my old tutor? Where have I
gone? His breath
is not mine.
I breathe in his
air, his scorn.

               He has all-
ready   disappeared into arche
                type

invading my room
with a power I   He didn't know he had till
didn't know he had.   he claimed
mine.

My breath stops.

Wherever I do not attend, he is
        whispering: "I
                    am who you might have been."
                [could have...   echoes should have]

He started Aikido   young
        mastering breakfalls,
                toppling with learned grace.

Flaunting power and proper ease, he
        taunts: "You too could have climbed to
                            Tenth Dan if...."

Instead I am this   woman
        trying against a cage of aging bones.

MAAI in Japanese means
        the distance between us, territory, space and

I exhale eschewing
        him   to fall flat
                        on the mat   and push up
            again.

Sister-Ship

After visiting with my sister Joan & family in Florida.
For my niece, Nathalie

By the sea we sat
Scrying the mirror of our youth
Trying to retrieve meaning and more
Watching a heaving sea, pelicans at work
Ploughing through waves of nostalgia
In our sister-ship
Making up time lost but never wasted

Two little girls
Another time, another place
By the same sea, too long ago
Looked back, amazed
We cared enough to spy them out
They jumped aboard and we made four
Dancing down life's vagaries
Making meaning at last

Sails fully unfurled in a good sweet wind
Mast tall against an autumn sky
Exploring mysteries that must remain
Negotiating inlets, avoiding storms
Remembering that treasure still unfound
Until the present brought us back
And four to two we back became
Until the next time we set sail our sister-ship

Another Northern Passage
Some Thoughts On Passing Through
from the Old Country to California

Canada in her cold mode makes Miami more appealing

Though a bitter wind may bite but there's a blue sky, right?
Out in the countryside across the horizon
                                        a seamless stretch of corn-stubble
Lies sleeping beneath a white winter duvet
But back in the big city backstreets lie belly high
                                        with Xmas leftovers
City-slickers slip slide slog
      through soggy slush, dive into overheated Tim Hortons, Second
                                        Cups and Starbucks
Backing out to howling gusts backed-up traffic exhausting,
                                        clutching streams of southern delight
A super-northern species sporting bright lightweight jackets
Traded in for toonies[1] after Hogmanay[2,]
                                        maybe from Hudson's Bay, eh?
But who remembers *les voyageurs* dealing in grave blankets[3]?
Unsimple lives criss-cross a-cross time:
Where a few dogsleds were, snowmobiles blow by,
Carts with steaming horses, now 4-wheel drives say it all
Canada's own Big Damn Cold Candy Apple,
                                        keeping warm in a mall.

Yet another northern passage from Old World to New
Driving east with Robert Q to catch a flight west
Watching flocks of funny flags, multiple maple leaf sandwiches[4]
Maybe-metaphors for ancestral blood boiled well in
                                        Keridwen's[4] kettle,
O Canada, my home and native land,
Call me back some summertime
Then my true patriot love perhaps you can command

1 Unbelievably, 'Canadian' for the two dollar coin.
2 Hogmanay: Scottish New Year.

3 *Les Voyageurs* were men employed by fur companies in Canada to carry goods and supplies. There is firm evidence that a policy of biological warfare against the indigenous peoples was carried out, notably by General Amherst in the 1760s; see *www.ualberta.ca/~nativest/pim/ClashofWorlds.html*, in which the natives were given blankets from smallpox hospitals to infect them with the then-fatal smallpox.
4 At least we got one of our own. Before it was a flag it might have been some food product icon.
5 Keridwen, Celtic Goddess of the Cauldron/Death/Rebirth.
6 These lines include words and phrases from Canada's National Anthem.

Downtown TO[1]
For my daughter Kim-Ellen

Where
Grandmother Nell, mother of mothers, in the prime of life, bled to death in 1939 saving money by not going to the hospital to bear her seventh, unlucky child, leaving six and her husband to a life-time of trauma, realizing what they had lost
Where
Dad, warrior fallen from grace, walked his last bridges after count-less ones at sea, though he lives still in the faces of too many home-less men hunched over coffee in run-down cafés
Where
Aunt Thel, family matriarch and martyr, dreamt soft pipe dreams whilst Stelco[2] made hard money on the real thing
Whence
Mom, erstwhile adventuress, escaped but doesn't have the heart to say when we track down old dead childhood friends
For whom
My sister sang in vain "a street's for feet" whilst cars careen, trams trundle by, till she too fled to Florida to sleep by the sea, saving her little family from death by pollution[3]
Where
My dedicated daughter, raised to solve the problems of our age, holds a vision of a better world at bay[3]

1 Toronto, Canada
2 She worked for long selfless years as the head filing clerk at the pipe/steel manufacturer Stelco's downtown Toronto headquarters.

3 My sister's husband and daughter suffer from MCS: Multiple Chemical Sensitivity
4 Bay St: a major downtown street, not far from where Kim lives and works. As a Gay/Pride activist she works for civil rights, but she also keeps a part of herself 'at bay' from it all.

Joan Marilyn and Me
For my sister Joan & brother-in-law Henri

Joan Marilyn and me,
Long ago we lived down by the sea
When life seemed to stretch out so infinitely

Together we dreamt in a tall room under a maritime moon
Over wind and waves, two little girls in two big beds
Soft white sheets and downy pillows over our heads

She was large and I was little
And though we liked to play
We grew up and fell away

But many years later we managed to meet
One sunny day on a summerhappy street
Car-free radicals dancing on committed feet[1]

Her smile full of our childhood
So familiar, so faraway,
Only she can bring the years and tears back that special way.

1 My sister and her radical comrades are responsible for the 'Streets are for Feet' Project in Toronto.

*Henri, Joan
and my niece Nathalie*

In the Meadow of My Youth

For my youngest brother, Ian

In the magic meadow of my youth
Tall grasses grow, birch and sumac glow,
Crab apples cook in sweet October's sun
Cornflowers call out concerning blue jays,
Bearing messages about other better days.
Bullrushes prosper, bare bushes prickle,
Muddy footprints bring back where I belong

This path took me too many times to count
Through canopy of trees and deep designs,
A place between the House Where Hunger Dwelt
And Hutton School, where once a clear stream ran
And strawberry fields captured our delight,
Before gas stations, high rises, fast food, the blight,[1]

Here in this little wood faeryland lived on,
Trolls and elves peered out from gnarled trunks
Gnomes came out to play, remember they?
Whispers of adventure lifted our hearts
And though suburban housing closes in,
Fences casting shadows on the ground
The magic of the place still holds true
The meadow, a measure and a clue

I did not find my pear tree there today
Perhaps it found a place in paradise with Pan
And little brother could not come with me
He wanders deep within his forest of despair
But I will take him there tomorrow, someday, soon

We will stretch high to take what life has given
That little golden apple on a spindly tree
A perfect metaphor for our immortality
He will smile like he used to, long ago
When we wandered in this meadow all aglow

With the nature of God, the mystery of The All
Responding to a universal spiritual call

All this and more the meadow means to me
It will always live within my child heart
Planted deep inside where'er I go, wild and free

1 Since the writing of this poem in October 1996, developers finally dismantled
the remnants of this 'meadow of my youth' in London, Ontario, Canada. The
nature spirits have fled. So much work needs doing to save such simple, magi-
cal places.

It Seems Like Yesterday
For Aunt Thelma

It seems like yesterday when I was twenty-one,
Ready for the road well traveled,
Instead I took back routes to hinterlands,
Breaking trails with a little help from friends

Now, lost hippies look cross as we drive by
In my daughter's sleek black Civic,
Dreams doomed in a military industrial complex
We hoped would die before our day was done

It seems like yesterday when I was thirty-one
Old as now my daughter's soon to be
Abandoning mediocrity to take a pilgrim's path
Peering through cracks to newagedom

Then Dad died, waving goodbye to new mother me
Through the windows of a train going West;
Wandering was what he did do most and best
His work was done, said Uncle Ralph,
                          who might have been a doctor if he could.

It seems like yesterday when I was forty-one
Love left me growing old, so calling forth the gods
One wish was granted I still am walking on
The path of relationship, beyond the sex and games

By then Aunt Thel had left for service on the Other Side,
But such a sadness stays, life's never been right since
She stopped cleaning, putting things away,
Come home sweet angel, I have so much to say.

It seems like yesterday when I was six years old
Or three or two or wading in the womb
Awaiting entry to a world at war
So, time's a god: careening between his traffic cops,
                          years hitting broadside or right on,
We face his cronies disease and death, minute meter maids,
                                      greed and speed,
Learn what we need, pass on what we cannot manage.

In the Woods of Venus

For my Dad and Joachim, lover long lost but never forgotten

See, that was me, that skinny teenager
Trekking home through snowy nights
The orderly suburban streets of London Ontario,
Kitted out in a heavy navy-issue great-coat[1],
Ready for battle, before night buses ran to Oakridge Acres,
Before the Bay of Pigs, before things changed.

Determined to be strong, hide despair, ride out failure,
Studying hard to be A First a close second unlikely third
Brainy brown-noser
Motivated to move up from the middle-class morass,
Whilst girlfriends wanted desperately to be wives,
Their freckled faces filled with worry about how and when.

Dark and different, my Lithuanian friend
Suspect in her smooth Cadillac convertible,
An audacious outsider, her hefty hardworking parents spoke survival,
Their overly odiferous basement boasting big barrels of sauerkraut
                                                    and pickles,
Damp black bread and thick sausages, worlds away from
An unenthusiastic Anglo-Canadian drive to the normalcy of
                                                    mac and cheese.

We'd put on high heels and dance at the German Club or drive
                                        up to Ipperwash Beach
Where we'd meet older men and drink beer by the lake,
Lonely Latvians, Lithuanians, yearning Yugoslavians,
                                        disgruntled Germans,
Remaking spoiled lives in The White North's hostile wilderness,
Picking tobacco under a hot sun or waiting tables in Toronto.
One loved me so he sang love songs and got Grace green with envy.

A babe in the woods of Venus,
Understanding little, mostly nothing,
I watched them kick soccer balls desultorily round Springbank Park,

*Leona and her
friend Grace (right)
as teenagers*

Finally marrying mercifully amongst themselves,
                                    fearing unknown alternatives
Or rejected too many times by sensible girls in saddle shoes,
               streamlined for a lawyer, doctor or mayhap a steel magnate
                                         from Hamilton.

They seemed deep and mysterious,
Tempting apples on my tree of life
I carried them home carefully wrapped up,
Gifts to test my mother's vaguely liberal gut.
A big secret was Johnny Vertika from Yugoslavia
But the most entrancing of all was Joachim of Leipzig
Who came for Christmas. My Animus King.,
We loved across dividing lines of two World Wars.

Dad was drinking at the downstairs bar he'd made in the rec room;
Leaning over menacingly at my Teutonic Adonis,
All blonde and beautiful,
Calling him Jerry, he challenged his old enemy to battle
For the heart of his dark daughter.

Was this what he had fought and died for,
To see his daughter end up with a Nazi?

Jack was still around when my sister married her gay Acadian
from Montreal.
He traveled to Ottawa all the way from TO to show he loved
the schoolgirl grown-up, gone to university,
He was my most courageous, he'd faced his demons when he'd
escaped across the Wall.
We might have married but I woke up
When he forcibly washed lipstick off my young face under a
bathtub tap

Nonetheless, I've never really kicked this addiction
to noble savages, rainbow warriors, outlaws,
this urge to confront wilderness in the mirror
to smell Iron John's sweet sweat
to fill full of oak and pine, sky and wind.

1 Navy/military term for a large heavy overcoat

Leona's father on board ship, probably 1930s.

The Streets of Toronto
For Grandmother Nell

On the streets of Toronto family ghosts stalk the living.
When we pass the old cemetery on Queen
They speak from out the grave:
Was it worth it, the misery of emigration? We had no choice. No, we
had choice but few if any options. And it was a potent dream, the New
World, that things would be better, that we might make it. We had
hope. For us of The Clearances and The Famine, it was the best way
out besides death. What we didn't know overwhelmed us when we
reached our destination, not to speak of the terrible passage across. And
whenever we got the chance, some of us went back to make sure our
children remembered, that we were remembered.
More often than not they wished they'd stayed at home,
In their dying moments
Out of touch with an earth, a stone, a tree, a walk, a house,
A loved one lost
Forgetting why they had left
In some nostalgic glaze remembering
The face of their old gran,
The grey stone croft their pappy's pappy grew from,
Cold feet all the days of their lives
Even in boiling sultry August heat
The difference between making it or not, so close, too far.
They trusted that we would count their cost
But memories faded,
The stories and songs by new hearths untold
Though now *rootsweb.com* and its ilk
Indicate a massive comeback,
Too late for the feeling, language lost,
Stories buried in too many unmarked graves
Not to speak of the bad, the impossible,
The forgivable unforgivable non-relationship
With the native peoples of this old new world

Winters on Toronto's streets signify too well mortality
The snow the ice the hail the wind the slush the rain
            the doughy cloud the long months into longer years

Until a lifetime is spent
Rich man, poor man, rag man, give a guy a bone
Before he fell down dead and no-one raised a stone,
A pauper's grave.
Pedlars, butchers, laborers, Church of England/Anglican,
                    Roman Catholic, Wesleyan Methodist...
The 1871 Ontario census lists them coldly but their stories
Fly out from between the lines, the letters...
They fought back—building, rebuilding in the image
Of what they'd unwillingly abandoned[1]
Unto this day they do, recreating bright little shops,
Barefaced reborn five-and-tens[2]
Ubiquitous corner coffee shops replacing ubiquitous banks,
Flashy bars, brave bistros,
Innumerable cosmopolitan, pricey renovated downtown condos,
Tall skinny mansions for gay wise city souls.
Still, they walk in the dead of night,
Stand in windows lit with fluorescent light,
Hunch over coffee cups, bundle up
Against it all but for it all with a vengeance.
Even the homeless take pride in coping,
Assuring the homey ones who give, they'll be alright
For the streets of Toronto were never for the faint of heart.

1 eg: London Ont sports a Thames River (with swans), Oxford Street and Hyde
   Park Road – not to mention nearby Stratford on the River Avon
2 Stores, like American five-and-dime stores...

*Leona and Kim (right)
at Grandmother Nell's
grave in Toronto*

The Cold Canadian Experience
For Michel Coté

is
taking mom to Canadian Tire to have her block heater connection reconnected
      waiting in a Tim Horton's coffee-cum-donut shop on a wintry solstice day
      hoping it's a smoke-free zone otherwise the donuts taste like smoke
      right?

seeing stretches of corn-stubbled fields up against a white cloud sky and
      remembering myself as a citizen of the world not an American after all whilst the
      world abroad fades against the foreground of scotch pine and memories of a
      fifties' youth spent full of sadness in regard to the
      possibilities of the human condition
      little did I know?

being rescued in a howling February mode when mom's Chevy went dead at Starbuck's
      by a French Canadian whose jumper cables didn't work but another English
      Canuck's did—all the same, it's coming to the rescue that counts
      eh, what?

slipping ass-up outside the homestead's front door on ice and thinking to have escaped
      injury so paying for it later by driving twice a week for 6 weeks to Beverly Hills
      to the best chiropractor on the planet
      you know what I mean?

buying WD40 just in case along with coarse salt and lots of heavy duty windshield fluid
      and fancy tough new windshield wipers AFTER I got caught on the 401 not
      being able to see a bloody thing with useless old California-dried up wiper blades
      and frozen fluid that a service island Brit employee kindly unfroze with 2 cups of
      boiling water
      enough, eh what, right?

On the Bus

*For Betty and Margaret on the occasion of driving up to Toronto from
London on the CAW (Canadian Auto Workers) bus for the Protest
March against the Conservative Ontario Government, October 26,
1996*

Margaret shares her life in the car industry, online old style,
Betty's succulent Scots accent charms us all the while
And I, old hippy out-of-towner, come home

Around us, sleeping men listen,
They love so much, we who sustain
What they work for, beauty, wisdom, truth

In another age they died on battlefields for us,
In this they carry flags that say they would,
We women who win the worst, the best

One of us was lucky not in love but she was true
One has come so long to say what's on her heart
One makes mistakes with men, adores them too

All three of us mother in more ways than one
We want to send a message, not leave The Work undone,
And so we troop our colours, together we sing old songs

We carry with us all the joy of being just of heart
The happiness that comes with caring as an art
The pride that passeth prejudice and heals the soul

We are the women of the world who save the trees
Who bind the wounds of those whom government deceives
Win the confidence of angels and *we* sleep well at night

---

*Opposite: Goddess over Glastonbury Tor by Jan Billings. Reprinted by
permission from "Offerings" by Anna Shaw and Jan Billings.*

In the Waiting Room of the Goddess
Solstice 2000
*For my dear friend Evelyn Isbister, in remembrance of
one of the most joyful people I have ever known*[1]

Here
In the Waiting Room of the Goddess
Snow falls thick and perfect
Winter winds whip cross continents
Ice gathers on trees and telephone poles
Sirens howl in the distance as aging generations
Stumble and pass away before an unlikely spring.

There
On the Other Side
She awaits us, holding in her hand a winged codicil
Containing all the mysteries we have forgotten to remember
Through passages of times, truths so vast, so glorious
Only the dying mind can embrace as light streams forth,
Beauty so wondrous, only the recovered soul can see.

Now
I wait my turn in the line-up, in this interlude
Between forms of service, between here and there,
Not merely life and death, death and rebirth,
But the tasks at hand, how we spend our daily lives
With family and friends, comrades in arms
The ordinary passages we make our own.

Then
She surveys my resume, my willingness to be a part
Of some intricate strategy for the betterment of all
Consults with gods of knowing who hover and spin
Like dervishes, in a passion of loving,
A divine taskforce at Her command,
And His, Her Consort, Ancient of Days.

Light
At Solstice through the darkened passageway comes
Pointing not only to right rhythms of nature and ritual
But to the eye/I who sees and thus can know
To act aright, to move with purpose through the veils,
To embody the Will of the Gods with our willing consent
Re-making all things new, making all the waiting worth-while.

1   Evelyn came to stay with my Canadian family and myself over Christmas
    2000 and New Year. The following March she went into a coma and passed
    away in May. She was truly in The Waiting Room of the Goddess.

Britain

In Memoriam
Read by Leona at Margaret Elen's funeral on October 18, 2001

*The Elen extended
family, 1989.
L to R: (Rear) Richard &
Leona, Frankie, John &
Kate, Kathryn; (Center)
Margaret & Bill Elen;
(Front) Kathryn's sons
Mark & Simon*

An English woman, good to the core
Who watched the world through gentle eyes
Wanting the best, having made the best choices
A woman of culture could make;
A professional woman who married an equal,
An English man, good to the core
Who loved, honoured and respected her.

Together they chose four
To raise, hold and have as kin
In a post-war era when socialism was the righteous way,
Their values were the best of Britain
The finest legacy they could leave

Beneath her quiet dignity
A great heart beat out eighty-five years of service
To students, family and friends
And the wider world in need of this natural nobility
That only such a good woman is capable of
It is good to remember now
In this time of trouble
That This Great Generation
Comprised in equal parts, women and men,
Born together to walk together
Through the valley of the shadow of death
Into the light of peace, reason and hope for humanity

Surely, all the days of our lives,
Margaret and Bill would want us to do likewise.

Women's Vote
By my friend, Margaret Kimber, "Wise Crone"

Take away men's franchise,
Take away their vote,
Take away the guns,
Reduce him to a bloke.
Give Women a thousand years to rule
See what mistakes they make.

Women running governments,
Businesses and schools,
Deciding who is boss,
Writing all the rules.
Give Women a thousand years to rule
See what mistakes they make.

Women learning to be strong,
Learning to run the game,
Using men as we were used
Pawns without the fame.
Give Women a thousand years to rule
See what mistakes they make.

Where would we find ourselves
A thousand years from now?
Would we have learnt from history?
Worship the sacred cow?
Give Women a thousand years to rule
See what mistakes they make.

Would life be just, and balanced?
Would truth win the prize,
Would money drive us crazy
Or might we be more wise?
Give Women a thousand years to rule
See what mistakes they make.

If we had a thousand year experiment
Of total matriarchal power
Would we have learned to value
The beauty of a flower
The need for clean air to breathe
For food without GM grains
Schools which teach life skills
Non-polluting planes
Give Women a thousand years to rule
See what mistakes they make.

I do not know how we would fare
If given half a chance
We need to change our minds around
Before we can advance.
Give Women a thousand years to rule
See what mistakes they make.

*Meggie
with her big
sister Muffin*

A magnetic poem about her mother by Muffin/Robyn

An angel saw me home/to my mother/I love her so/the flower of
light/the music if whispered/and a butterfly flying together/with
yellow day/dark night/red dreams and/all believe/how magic is
her glow

Ladies of the Commonweal:
Wise Crones A-Waiting[1]
On Awaiting the Birth of my Goddess-Daughter
Megan Poole Kimber at Hornblotton House, Somerset, April 1996
For Margaret, Muffin, Meggie and Fiona Nairn-Scott (pictured)

We, the Ladies of the Commonweal,
Awaiting the birth of a New Queen,
Walk the misty Courts of Avalon,
All knowing the needs of her future
Green and golden, full of goodness.
Black Queen, regal Isis cloaked
Who was before the Nile's flow,
Dark, waist-long tresses, bronze face aglow
Instead of hero Horus
Her womb holds every woman's hope.[2]

Red Queen, Elizabeth revealed
Rightful ruler of realms north and south
By bloody mix of veins,
Unruly red head, dragon angel-heart
Who fashions wings for us to fly.[3]

White Queen, Guinevere undone
Of Otherworldly fame
Wandering this world's magic isles,
Seeking her own kind
Solutions to the problems of her age.[4]

We haunt Hornblotton's hallow'd night,
Hooded against a cold moon, counting stars,
We come upon the stables bright
With Peter Potter's fire-full-kiln
Bursting to yield its wingéd charge.

Whilst down in her deep sea castle
Our wee Mermaid Queen
Stirs to see this augured passage
Of eagles[5] bred from Scorpio clay

Time to come forth and play this starry eve, this waking day.

1 In 1992 Margaret and I co-founded the Wise Crone Café (pictured above) at the Glastonbury Festival of Performing Arts to raise money for 'worthy causes.' This Good Work has continued under her command.
2 Margaret Kimber: mother of Maiden Muffin, at 48 birthing Mermaid Megan. English but born in the Far East, carrying that aura.
3 Fiona Nairn-Scott: Wise Crone, aeronautics engineer; English/Scottish,
4 Me!
5 Peter the Potter/Sculptor was taking his turquoise eagles from the kiln. They symbolize the Eagle/Scorpio part of the Glastonbury Zodiac where Hornblotton House (the estate) lies.

Seahorses

By my friend, Marianna Lines 'The Lady of the Stones'

Like tiny black threads
Floating in a tank
One squints at the illusion of reality
Are they really
Tiny black creatures
Baby seahorses of the snowdrop spring
Headliners in the St. Andrews Citizen
Wee Fifers all seven
Sea life nursery in St Andrews
Aussie parents, Scottish born
Will they vote for independence
When the parliament opens
Will they wear a kilt and drink whisky
Only now can they lightly float
And kink their backs
One stretch and they are a real miniature
Of a seahorse
One flex and they are a tiny thread of life
An elderly visitor watched them for a few long minutes
Then spoke to his Mrs.
"They've got a long way to go" he said
and shook his head sadly
The spikey parents link tails
Pretending they know all about Pictish art
On stones
Especially at Alberleno

Lady of the Stones

For Marianna Lines, author of Sacred Stones, Sacred Places

There she lives, the Lady Marianna,
Within the enchanted circle of Scathach's stony realm
Of green swaths and purple heathers,
Scrubby bush and mirror scrying pools

In old Collessie, where beached selkies
Dream of seas not far away;
Mayhap Finn McCool passed this way
On his journey through these sov'reign isles

Here Cailleach Bheur, blue-faced hag
Holds her winter games, till Blessed Brigit
Comes to claim back the springtime
Of youth, when wrens and robins sing

And sparrows dance, in memory of Mabon
And Mother Madron, beloved Lady,
Before Ninian walked or Columba converted,
So sad their songs at Calvin's coming

Out there, in that fine field,
A farmer, long dead, dropped
The seed to feed his family, left
The stone sleeping, flat on his tattooed back

Awaiting the touch of my lady dear
Who wakens stones to tell their tales
Amongst a worthy folk who wield
A past still shadowed in their wake

Lady of the Stones, Maid of Miracles,
Betrothed of Somerled, lord of these lands,
Daughter to Muirlearteach, Mermaid Queen,
She serves the past and future well, her gift

Out Standing

An English Country Garden Revisited

On trimming the little garden at our house in Somerton, Somerset,
August 1997. For Angela and her mother Gloria Langdon,
gardeners extraordinaire, and Angela's husband Ron

Ten years ago an English country garden
Enchanted me with the possibility
Of all that might have been but has not come to pass
So I have come home to you uprooted
Uprooting all that ought not be
Before returning back across the sea

Still, I feel a longing to have lived
What might have come my way
Before heading for the broad and busy highway
A world too wide for comfort
Falling westward into chasms of adventure
Leaving what might have been with you

I did abandon you to those who care not
For the careful teachings of an English country garden
But now return to perform this happy penance
To listen to the wisdom of what might have been
Forgetting not what passed ten years about
Five with you in happiness and five without
You might have made of me an Englishwoman
Full, round and rosy-cheeked, briar-sweet
Rooted deep, blossoming honeysuckle
And white hawthorn hedge. You turned in time
Into a sorry tangle, tiny pond gone dead,
Forcing frogs abroad to search a finer clime

But you must needs forgive me as I bend
Upon my knees to bring you back to rights,
Turning your sod back up to the light,
Disciplining would-be elders in your midst,
Giving Richard's rosebush reason for rebirth
And planting pretty pots along your stony girth
The tulips and the daffodils I cannot stay to see
But will remember mum's geraniums

Angela & Ron

And the pear tree that first brought you to me
A new friend says he's pulled memories from the walls
But mine are stored safely in this garden heart
Now bring me back to make another start.

Five White Geese
After having chosen Aphrodite on a goose
from an ancient Greek design for our Wise Crone Café T-shirt

Outside my window
Behind the foreground
Of an ever-prolific hedge
Of dark fruiting elder
Five white geese wander
Clearly outlined
On a verdant English pasture
They strut and straddle
Preen and waddle
Back and forth, fluttering
Their wings like angels
Considering flight
But thinking better
They line up in formation
Five beauties remindful
Of Love's Sovereignty

Disappearing off to the right
Of my line of vision
Through a wonderland
Dropping golden eggs
By lucky ducks like me
Transforming into maidens
Going whither they will
Oh Sweet Aphrodite
Your messengers multiply
As I pass through
This pretty paradise
Be kind to me
In the land of love
For you
Are
Queen

The Goddess Work
One for Kathy Jones, Mistress of Avalonian Mysteries

In Avalon, not so long ago
                    Two sisters sat down in one's kitchen
Redolent of every woman's will
                    With glasses of wine and conversation
That turned the tide of patriarchy
                    Like witches real and imagined
We practiced The Old Craft
                    Evoking, invoking, making, remaking
Calling up Her Cone of Power
                    Bringing Our Lady back home to us
Red, White and Black
                    Now She walks amongst us once again

India

Womb of Wonder
For Conrad M. (pictured)

In the Womb of Wonder
She surrounds me, Mother India
Sends me magical dreams down her long peace pipe to the gods
Watches me watch cockroaches
Listens to me listening to rats in the dry corners
                    of my soul-wise journey here

Where the monsoon floods us with walls of rain
Through which we watch long-necked birds catch deep-eyed fish
Their caw cawing and pretty pretty sounds
                              taking up our wilting hearts
Into the glowering skies.
By Ganesh's sacred lake

64

We work on the wilderness of our ways[1]
Pit patter our fingers along ant running keys
Printing off an ant colony crushed on virgin tree paper
The oil-based plastic PCs bringing paradox home to bear

The thought of all this weighs down my uncivilized soul
Awaiting the divine revelation
Of
How
To
Stop
It
All

1 I was part of the group
  working on putting
  together the 6th World
  Wilderness Congress in
  Bangalore, India,
  October 1998

With Toda elders

From Bandipur Park, South India

You are the masters here, in this world
They await you there in the Other
We walk unwillingly in your footsteps, having forgotten our pathway
But we are re-membering our selves and we awaken at your risk

Pretending we hold the power behind your back we delude ourselves
We don't like it hate to admit any of it
And many are beyond caring, real women[1] for lost men

Determined to redefine ourselves
We watch you doing your best and worst, saving the planet, selling arms
Struggling to walk white mighty amongst brutalized brown negated black
The hope of western civilization in digitalized eyes
Whilst on the sidelines waiting for their moment yellow turns to gold

We the women who bear you could change it so quickly but never do
Instead too often we trek one, two, three behind
Though you may carry our bags and let us follow you through sliding
doors into corridors of power

Some say we sacrifice our femininity but it's more a question of figuring out the game and changing the rules, if we could, and we might, in time

Here, unsuited in the East,
We are defined by you, what you have made of this world
Whilst in the West we bear the trappings of patriarchy

Be gentle merciful as your white sun sets, for it is
As we love envy and support you we share your fate
With angry elephants dispossessed tigers tribals who beat drums all night
To ward off evil spirits, white ghosts who plague the planet

Our guys, do your best *lest in the Other World we suffer worse*

1 A reference to the development of the right wing 'real women' anti-women movement.

After India
For Mike Jones

After India
everything's too clean too efficient too full of easy exits too on time
even here in British Emperial disorder

After India
the mind's eye seeks serious satisfaction
in mighty deeds to be done, having been made aware of the
larger dimension
the soul emerges re-engaged to vision

III: Owl In Ojai

Owl in Ojai
For Lee S.

Ojai was a haven, a coming home
The place where angels placed me
A waiting room of the gods

And did the myth of Bloeduwedd[1]
Return to take another twist:
Made by a magician, cast away?

Indeed, I was an owl in Ojai
Watching through the night
Hunting out my prey, desires

That, uneaten, undigested,
Stand in the way of flight
To places further in the heart.

In the day outer work
Became me, though it's a sleep
Compared to inner work

But with the dark I slipped
Away, to find the mastery
Of love, which patience is

Trees were home enough,
A branch, an arm which holds
A body, leaves my disguise

My friends, those other birds
From tribes returning to their souls
With stories from the wars to tell
And for all that, I am an owl still
Loosed from bonds of men magic
To take my fill, fly high as I will

*Lee with Cheetah
Conservation Fund
ambassador Chewbaaka
in Namibia*

1 In this Brythonic myth Bloeduwedd, made of flowers by a magician for his magic hero nephew, falls in love with one of her own choice; eventually she is turned into an owl. In *At Home in Bell Buckle* I used this myth to describe a friend's way of being: 'Made All of Flowers She Was.'

Yo Beato[1]

By my friend, Nan Tolbert (pictured)

There lives in upper Ojai
A lady of fine stories
Shocking and bright
She and they delight.

Many's the time her twinkling eyes
Sparkle our hearts and fancies,
Ever reaching mirth's very core
Ever playing truth's own games.

Her voice singing,
She handles clay,
Inspiring us
Throughout the day.

What more may a friend do?
Offer chocolate?
    Tease?
        Share gifts?
This lady does!
While we learn of thanksgiving,
    Of beauty.

1 Nan, co-founder of the Ojai Birth Resource and Family Center, developed a very special relationship with the renowned philosopher-Queen and mistress of clay, Beatrice Wood ('Beato'). Since the writing of this poem Beato passed away (March, 1998).

Oestre Angel In Ojai
For Veda Lee, newborn, March, 1998

Today an Oestre[1] angel
Drifted down morning clean streets
Across a waking valley
Fresh from wild gorges and clearing streams,
Chaparral treed steep slopes and hawkeyed peaks
A messenger from Ojai's mountain guardians
Sporting an ever new springtide cloak of wonders,
Lilies blooming, tulips before their time,
Real bunnies running for life
Whites and pinks and yellows, purples too,
Eggs of all sorts opening to possibilities,
Peace and plenty and pretty babes all in a row.

1 'Easter' originates from the Germanic 'Oestre', goddess of springtime, eggs, the
pagan roots of the Christian celebration.

Leona's mother, Florence, on the streets of Ojai

Black Man Out Of Brooklyn

On the Occasion of Dealing with 56 Boxes of Wine
from Cheetah Valley, South Africa

I met
The Black Man Out Of Brooklyn
Down on Highway 150
His rig so big and shiny
Never saw the like in Ojai, ever

Box after box we unloaded
Remembering who we were all along
We spoke of white men, he sang his song of liberation,
The white American male an evil phantom to be exorcised
The white American female a mean-spirited money-minded witch
He let me off his hook, Canadian and part native as I may be,
Like his lost Parisian lady, a kind of wild winged thing

When things got too intense, I threw spirit into the mélange
He drew back into the nature of his kind
Leaving me bereft, a little down
For he was a Harley-Davidson man
Brought back memories of Gene the Marine
Long ago, travels down from BC
Through the apple orchards of that spinning youth
If he'd've asked just right, maybe I might have left,
Driven clear cross country to Brooklyn
And re-invented my own American Dream

I Belong to the Gods
For Diana B.

When I look into the mirror of myself
Where Alice-Mae[1] still runs amok
Through the wonderland of eternal youth[2]
An amazing Beauty beams me back,
Otherworldly, untouched by mundane men,
For I belong to the gods[3], and they my fate do form.
Now, round about, a near impregnable cage
Protects unmarried[4] me from men made in some lesser image.
Husbands, mayhap two too many[5], lovers all in a row,
Fade away, whilst the gods loom bright before me.
From their pinnacle they hover, figuring my fate
Ringing pass-nots round this prison sweet
So do I spin and twirl round the fingers
Of those living gods in whom I have some trust
That they do live and touch the little minds of men.[6]

1 Alice-Mae: my middle 'christened' name, for my paternal Grandmother Alice
  Taylor and aunt Edna Mae.
2 My first real job, age 15, was at Wonderland Gardens in London, Ontario!
3 Poetic license: includes goddesses...
4 Written during a difficult, 'unmerry,' time when I became 'unmarried' for a
  second time
5 The gods may be jealous (as only gods can) of most husbands of 'daughters of
  men' they choose to protect and prefer them to remain 'wise virgins' in the
  ancient sense: independent women. Twice legally divorced, I return to the
  path of partnership—this the gods also advise.
6 The Great Invocation: "Let purpose guide the little wills of men".

View of the Ojai Valley

Ojai Gals

For, amongst so many, Lee, Mo, Nan, Paddy, Dale and Therese

I celebrate
The Ojai Gals of Old
Those Otherworldly Queens
Like Annie Besant & Beatrice Wood
Keepers of golden cords between the worlds
Who surely over-light the New, living this-world queens
Marys, Marthas & Magdalenes, Valley of the Moon Madonnas
Withstanding golden girls of Fernando, Bernardino, Silicon &
Other Valleys of Deceit. When met in LA dens & studios & Santa
Barbara bistros, messages pass & looks impart, for we Have kept
The Ojai, our beloved Shangri-La[1] apart . . . .

1 The famous Frank Capra Shangri-La movie called 'Lost Horizon' was partially
filmed in Ojai (1937).

The Green Queen
For Pat Weinberger, Ojai environmental and political activist

TriVia, Goddess of The Three Ways[1]

Overawe
Oversee
Overtake

Inaugurate
Infiltrate
Intimate

Through the dust of hot California summers
Riotous pleasures of unbelievable winters
Mysterious vagaries of sometime springs

She falls
Upon an innocent incomer
Green glory intact

The determined, dextrous, didactic, diligent nature of
Unmistakable Earth Mother, Wise Crone of the First Order

Under through it all she points a way
Opaque crystal in hand the amber liquid merely
Undermining lesser liquids of choice

She Is The Avenue to Main Street
She Who Built The Infrastructure of God Speed[2]
Carrying the Blood of Community to its River of Life

She plays us one for another
To elicit the Truth of the Matter At Hand
Having lost two angels to Death[3] she deals in Life Causes
As others fall, she rises again
Averring nothing of the falsely spiritual
Dealing with spirits who watch over her welfare

There is no end to her beginnings
But who can walk in her path after her approach
This Green Queen of the Valley of the Moon Goddess[4]?

1 Wise Crones amongst us say that
the Great Triple Goddess (*Tri Via,*
Three Ways) was insidiously trans-
formed by patriarchy to its oppo-
site, "the making of three or more
small issues."

2 I am informed by my knowledge-
able scholar of a mother that the
origin of the First Gossip is in
truth, God Speed, probably what
the proverbial Old Wives said as
they passed useful information on.

3 Sadly, Pat's daughter Rosalind R.
Dwight and her late husband Dr.
Laurence Weinberger.

4 One of the legends about Ojai is
that it is the Valley of the Moon,
and that 'Ojai' means Moon Nest.

Photograph by Cheri Barstow

The Oldest Profession Is Mothering
For Cheri Barstow and Michele Hansen

The oldest profession is mothering
Home maker, bread baker, care taker
Hearth keeper, love's reaper
Wears charms, bares arms
She warms, disarms
Humanity's house alarms
Go off
When she is less than all that she can be
Gather round, harvest in,
Blessed Be
First Lady of The Apple Tree

Ojai Poets
On the Occasion of Having Attended A Meeting of Poets in Ojai

March winds whistling up my ass
I sat down to a poet's fest, the test, to pass
A mind-swell of less than delightful dissection,
From prickly artichoke versus pear[1]
To the mischievous machinations of a Martian Chief,
A fulsome rebellion against minimalist LA black and pansy
studded salads,

A vision of a long line of American poets before my mind's-eye
Whitman foremost, Sandburg and Thoreau close behind,
Frost following up,
Maybe Neruda had a look-in and why not Dante after all?
I read long poems and short
Defended the House of Spirits[2]
Where still great Sappho sings and Emily too
Owned up to liking rhyme and forcing issues
For poets are not perfect, just sublime.

1 One for TS Eliot savants…
2 The title of the first poem in my last book of poetry, *At Home in Bell Buckle*

Left to right: Three mothers, Nan, Cheri and Mo

The Man With The Key to Death
For Mo

Yesterday
A man
Neither old nor young
Walked into the post office
Post box key in hand
A book tucked under his arm
Just near enough
For me to read the title
The Key to Death
Hell-bent on his personal postbox
He didn't see what I saw
All sorts of strange metaphors came to mind
You may imagine them.
Somehow it was just so Ojai
I had to poet it down to see what might happen.
Not much so far
But that's sort of what the experience was like
A peak moment that might have been but wasn't but could be
anytime now

Sisters at the Front
For Paddy and Janis, WILD colleagues

There comes a day when work becomes us sisters at the front,
We who work to live, who choose to live as well
Paths more benign than sisters who came before
Yet without whom we would be less than we are:
Women who can choose at all,
Who move from job to job, house to house,
From men unworthy to others or none at all.
So, though we sit before PCs, producing
More of what may be for good or ill —
For at the front issues of survival haunt us still
As we move through many war zones
Where meaning takes its toll upon the soul—
Finally we pass into the place of waking vision
Beyond merely enough or just getting plenty more,
We take into our hands the arms that free the mind,
The pay-packet less purport-full by day, as by night
We plan retreats and forages into deeper dimensions of delight
Where Beauty rules the day and Truth is now in sight.

The Magic of Ojai
For Alasdair Coyne and the environmental activists of Ojai

It might lie a little
With merchants, Council and Chamber,
A motley array of artisans, mercurial Mexican cafés,
An unsubtle suburb surrounding a pseudo-Spanish center
Where clumps of cloudy pilgrims, agape with brand names
Ponder paramount desires through fickle looking-glass facades,
In a predictable parade along The Avenue
Punctuated by clock and belltower's ringing notes,
Here, where many elderly come to expensive ends
Beyond the confines of The Little House[1]

But more likely it lies
Within an earthy spirituality,
Hallowed spirits of departed elders
Hov'ring above this Owl's Nest,
This Valley of the Moon Queen[2],
Like Krotona's[3] hierarchy who crown Our Town,
HPB, Krishnamurti and his benefactress Annie B.,[4]
Where the littlest grave diggers[5]
Prepare the earth for a century's millennial death,[6]
As The Age of Theosophy and World War
Yields to yet another New Age along the River of Tao

As now Beato[7] joins the gods . . .
But most truly the Magic of Ojai abides
In a sky blue barometer of light,
A desert heat that lifts the soul,
Majestic mountains round a valley surpassing superlatives,
Cloaked in purple ceanothus and sturdy chaparral,
Spring's rushing streams and hunting hawks,
Golden dust down long fiery summers,
Glorious gardens, venerable oaks inspiring melodrama,
Prolific pepper trees, orange blossoms and heady jasmine,
Here in One Very Long Ecstatic Happy Valley.[8]
But then again, magic, true to itself, lies mysterious,
Where it wills

1 Ojai's Senior Center associated with the busy, helpful charity, Help of Ojai.
   Many well-off elderly retire to Ojai.
2 Referring to some of the legends associated with the meaning of the name
   "Ojai".
3 Krotona Library and School, part of the Theosophical Society, situated high
   on a hill.
4 HPB (Helena P Blavatsky) and Annie Besant, Founder theosophists.
5 Ground squirrels/gophers had rather taken over the grounds.
6 Written in 1999.
7 Beato: Beatrice Wood, famous potter, dame extraordinaire and philanthropist
   who died days before this was written (March, 1998) *See page 68*.
8 The eastern part of The Ojai Valley; name of the Krishnamurti school and
   Foundation supported by Beatrice Wood.

Spindle of Fate
For Katie

An old-time Bohemian girl
A round woman in a square-peg world
To whom the gods speak, but gently

Twenty years wife mother confidant and friend
To one in particular, maybe a few too many
In the Name of Service

As she has loved many do before and after
Penelope at her tapestry, awaiting Ulysses' return
From proud journeys for his heart's desire

She mirrors my past
I reflect a future she may take or leave
We are every woman in her middle years

Spinner and weaver by nature, she faces outward
Into the maw of America, sensitivities honed,
Holding in her hand the spindle of the goddess of fate[1]

1 Of the three Greek Fates (the Moiroi or
Parcae), Clotho was the spinner, Lachesis
the drawer of lots and Atropos controlled
the inevitable end to life. Human fate
was spun around a person at birth by
these divine Spinners. They came to be
identified as a trio of older females who
handled the threads of human life, one
thread allocated to every person. Each
goddess took her turn in manipulating
this thread. Clotho selected, Lachesis
measured, and Atropos cut it to signify the
end of a person's existence.

Kate Martin and one of her creations

The Canyon Wren[1]
For Mary-Ellen McCabe

The canyon wren
Sings simply
To the heart

As the day draws down
Its shutters from the sky
She tipples up the pink champagne
Of night, her sweet tones
Mingling light to starry dark

Across the canyon other birds
Sit sleepily in live oak trees
Whilst she reminds us
Of the mystery Old Country sisters
Tended to with noble druids[2]

Hawks defend skies by day
Ravens and crows sail cross the sun
Whilst wee wren waits the coming
Of the time between before
Ojai Owl claims eventide her own

She sings of life's infinitesimal poignancies
Unwrit poems, unlived dreams
Underlying nature's magnitude and multitude
Underlining the importance of being small but beautiful
Or maybe just about being

1 Written when I was Program Director at the International Center for Earth
  Concerns in Santa Ana Canyon, Ojai
2 The wren was the most sacred of birds to the Celtic druids.

IV: Moon Over Topanga

There And Back Again
By my partner Richard

When I went off to have my "mid-life crisis", neither of us really thought that we would ever get back together. But having gone out, I started to come back, albeit via incomplete, yet sometimes instructive relationships – but I didn't realize that yet.

It took the magic of a particular piece of music to tip the scales. Whilst listening to one of the many Internet audio streams one day, up came an astonishingly beautiful piece – the Paul Winter Consort, from an album called *Celtic Solstice*, featuring many top-class Irish guest musicians. The song was a setting of W. B. Yeats' 1899 poem, *The Song of Wandering Ængus* (see following page). The arrangement, with pipe organ, saxophone and a heavenly female vocal, brought me to tears. With it came the realization that the only person in the whole world who could understand why this meant so much to me was Leona.

At the time, she was on the point of departing for Canada. Months passed. Finally, I came to realize that I had headed in the wrong direction in relationship. I asked for a miracle – and just before Christmas, 2000, there came an email from Leona's daughter Kim-Ellen, with her insight that the two of us had always been happier together than apart.

Being truly honest with myself, I had to admit that I was still deeply in love with Leona. We agreed to experiment with being together again – and the magic has worked! We are more conscious of how we value each other than before.

I am hopeful that the new clarity I have developed over the past couple of years will pay dividends in enabling me to grasp the real meaning of love and relationship. I thank Leona for taking the risk of getting back together with me, and for her forgiveness. I am committed, this time, to avoiding past mistakes and taking nothing for granted. And opening up new possibilities for us both.

The Song of Wandering Ængus
From "The Wind Among the Reeds" (1899),
by W. B. Yeats (1865–1939).

I went out to the hazel wood,
Because a fire was in my head,
And cut and peeled a hazel wand,
And hooked a berry to a thread;
And when white moths were on the wing,
And moth-like stars were flickering out,
I dropped the berry in a stream
And caught a little silver trout.

When I had laid it on the floor
I went to blow the fire a-flame,
But something rustled on the floor,
And someone called me by my name:
It had become a glimmering girl
With apple blossom in her hair
Who called me by my name and ran
And faded through the brightening air.

Though I am old with wandering
Through hollow lands and hilly lands,
I will find out where she has gone,
And kiss her lips and take her hands;
And walk among long dappled grass,
And pluck till time and times are done,
The silver apples of the moon,
The golden apples of the sun.

Leona and Richard together again – at Trethevy
Quoit, an ancient site in Cornwall, Britain
(August 2001)

Which Bird Is It?

A song by my friend & neighbour Lisa Salloux

Which bird is it, wakes me from a closed eye
      wakes up my ear, loud and clear.
With an early bird pattern, telling me about life
      in this old oak domain, where none's the same.

Onebody's stepping to twobody's door
      calling on threebody's dawn
        quelled by a finger on fourbody's shoulder
I'm five bodies here on my own.

Now that I'm alive, I let you flood in.
Your clarity pulls at my reckless beauty.
You've said a few words, you attend my hotel...
      when you're in the halls, walk well...I'm listening.

Onebody's guessing at twobody's story
      hoping for threebody's song
        compelled by a lick on fourbody's wrist
I've five bodies in me alone.

You're best in blue, son of nature be true
      in the end we rip off our temples.
Now guiding our souls, we still breathe in gold
      and pirate our way into virtue.
By the way, I noticed that somebody's listening,
      is there anything else you want known?
By the way, I noticed that somebody's glistening,
      is there anyplace else you want to go?

Onebody's talking to twobody's bones,
      while threebody lifts up the veil
      braced for the capture of fourbody's oil
      my bodies quiver to stone...
I quiver to stone.

A Harp at Six

considering impossible options
to evert[1] Valentine's Day
preparing to emigrate from this city of unlikely angels
besieged with lonely singles dysfunctional couplings
putting aside therapy dating services bar-hopping
in favor of poetry readings renting movies
hanging out with blue sky hawk and mountain peak
writing myself out of the tangle of trauma
I attend to a harp at six
off Ventura Blvd
its aboriginal notes lifting me
from out the craters of low life considerations

1 Seldom-used word for turning inside out (Transitive)

Topanga Messengers
For Caitlín, our cat from Tennessee

ants suffer us here in their high hills
wasps whiz around testing wills
mosquitoes mocking modern might
quake fire mudslide stalk day and night
coyotes catch incautious cats
big birds fly like acrobats
gods of this place
we share their space
if wise, with grace

Everyday Belongs to The Red Queen
For Donna T.

After the rain sun lights up the mountains, majestic,
                    standing tall, in robes of lush and glistening green,
Summer dry and fire fear distant memories
This is no winter, this benign mix of water light and shade
When much of Turtle Island shivers under ice, snow and
                                        steely wind

In the USA, today is Inauguration Day
Business goes on as usual
A serious gaggle of gifted men
Meander down the mountain to make money
At the Greatest Show On Earth. Women do too, of course,
But many Ladies of the Canyon keep their court at home,
Where clouds meet treetops and fog sweeps through chaparral

In California, everyday belongs to the Red Queen
And though we be Her Ladies-In-Waiting
Here in Her pretty palisades
Can we say what sort of entrance She might make?
With Her Coming the very ground gives way to immanence.
What will She claim as sacrificial tithing,
Queen of the Old School, direct in taking what is due?
Have we not eaten at Her table,
Treated Her temples with disrespect,
Polluted Her pleasure domes?

Descendents of men who followed stars westward ho!
And women dancing in the bitter streets,
We have reckoned the cost of California's taxes,
Taking the measure of mud storms, quake and fire,
But we all wait upon Her Ladyship's wrathful return.
After that the sun will shine again over Topanga

One for Brigit

This one's for Brigit
That fiery goddess behind the scenes
Whose water we drink, whose inspiration we seek

Are you that vast presence behind me, behind my eyes,
                     the way I see when I am clear,
The breeze that crosses my path and lifts
              the scent of jasmine through my world
Perchance, the hand that gently leads me
                when I am confused and tired
Or pushes when I resist what's right?

Perhaps, indeed, you are embodied in all I touch
You hide within so many names
Brigit, Bride, are only a couple I've caught
When your eyes met mine and you whispered in my ear

After all, what's a goddess to a mortal?
An inspiratrix, one who moves the mover
Who can be found in the smallest and the largest
She Who Brings Us Back In Time

Leona & Kathy – carrying out the Goddess Work in Glastonbury (1980s).

A Poem A Day
For Penn Kemp

a poem a day
holds demons at bay
doomy voices
limiting choices
proxy platitudes
deceptive dudes
pension phobia
market mania
the price of pig
who gives a fig?
modern Hades,
mix of shades
in Mammon's mirror
life proves dearer
here in the Real World
faery flags unfurl'd
we wander at will
scaling Yggdrasil[1]
truth abundant
shows killer cant,
wakes the witch wall'd in
with mystic Merlin
frees the fickle muse
to wonder, amuse
Taliesin sings
inspiration brings
Sappho sits on high
Poesy shall not die

1 The 'world tree' of Scandanavian mythology.

Days With Mother
For my mother Florence

Why is it
When we spend days together
I feel incomplete
As if we never do what we could
As if ever more needs doing?

I have not taken you everywhere
Shown you the glories of all this space and time
Nor said the needful things worth saying
To make it oh so perfect now and then
Not managed to be all to you
I would be to say I love you

As if something hangs between us

No matter what I do to make it clear
The mist drops down and we are moving along a dark river

Back into times gone by

When I was just a little girl you loved me so
In such a way I could say
My mommy loves me so she would mend the moon for me
When it breaks in pieces and wanes away

Such a mother comes once in lifetimes
No need to search another
So I mother many
Because you have been one for me

I fear the day you go
And leave me, not alone
But lonely, till we meet again
You do not want to go before me
Before any of your five bluebirds flown free
Circling inside the cage of your heart

Your apple pies will stay with us all the days of our lives
Your long smile and dark looks
That way you have of being more than you seem

Never like other mere mothers,
You were a friend growing with us in our peradventures
A person who played mother well

Jane Bowles
or, *On Considering Being Wife to Genius*

Jane Bowles
Wife of the infamous Paul 'Freddy' Bowles
Friend of Gertrude Stein and Bill Burroughs
Died in 1973
Incapacitated

Why do I think of that other wife
So faithful to her bitter end?
Vivian Eliot
Nemesis of Tom
Incarcerated

Wives to genius
Famed writers, movers of their times
Trend-setters now enshrined

The truth was more mundane
It always is
Even in the poetic dreamscape
Of Tangiers
Or Bloomsbury
Virginia didn't bother waiting for her bitter end
She invented it, embraced it: her Waves

Paul said Jane hated writing, only wrote to keep him,
                                        hid or wasted her work
Lest he trap it for posterity

She drank too much and lived for the day.
Was she black magicked?
In Morocco magic is as real as cyanide
Belief is All
The universe as we know is held together by Cherifa's cat[1]
Slinking round the corner
Was it black or does it matter, one of the kittens will be

Too many women wives to genius
Spinning in circus acts to bolster *joie de vivre*
Existentialist queens in youth, meant never to grow old
Famous after the fact for being who they were

1 A reference to the philosophical implications of Schrödinger's cat.
  "Schrödinger's Cat and Wigner's Friend/Lead to paradox without end..."

Spring in the Court of Calafia
For Renée Gander

Heralding the Court of Calafia[1]
Black and gold-eyed Susies in soft yellow cloaks
Sing of spring in The Red Queen's siren lands
Dancing in a wisp of wind
With royal purple lupins
Whilst golden poppies, like fire sprites
Come and go, here and there
Till finally The White Queen herself appears,
As the white blossoming yucca, food of old gods
Whilst heady scent of orange and jasmine
Send our senses into whirligigs of wonder

1 Calafia, referred to here and elsewhere, appeared in a 1510 romance by Garcia
  Ordoñez Montalvo, *The Sergas of Esplandian,* widely read by the Spanish
  invaders of the 16th century. In the book, she was the Queen (her name,
  sometimes seen as "Califa", might mean "female Caliph") of an island "very
  near to the Terrestrial Paradise", and at war with the Crusaders. According to
  Edward Everett Hale, and with good reason, this is the origin of the name of
  the State of California. See *The Queen of California,* Colt Press, San Francisco,
  1945.

Last Night's Dream
For Freida Myers

Did I dream
Three women went a-wandering
On an intrepid journey out of time
By subtle means of travel
Mind-matter transfer to places pivotal
For an unraveling of good and ill?
The lesson, ascertain reality.
As we left, our mystery task was done
(Its making turmoils my memory still)
Three men in black appeared, their purpose posed
Potential hazard of uncertain sort
Hidden, revealed, of three, I spoke our need
Did a deed of clarity, where Word was Power
We circled round some sleepy suburb scene
Where one house held three children dear to one
The face of that man in black, bearded,
Came through one, she fell from grace
To serve again
Whilst we two as three flew safely home
But where I cannot say
Lest it be here, high in the mountains where hawks fly.
When waking in the night
I spoke to him who watches over, his feather headdress
Shining in the night, his face an antique hue
There in that far place above where from
We work the midnight magic
But who was she who fell
And we who flew
What parts of me do so
And are the children us at any rate
And was this my youth my brothers two and me
Wendover Road so very long ago, the morning sound
Of horses on the street, the ragman passing by
Or was this all but hints of angels and Los Angeles?

But now I have seen his face

Moon Over Topanga[1]:
The White Queen's Will
For Lisa & Kurt—good friends make good neighbors

Here in the highlands of the Tongva[2]
The Old Ones hibernate under mountains, in caves,
Awaiting The White Queen's Will
They do not call the Moon Diana

Under her domain came
Jesus Santa Maria,[3] Topanga's primordial postman,
Elena Valenzuela from Lake Elsinore[4] to Garapatos[5]
To bear eighteen babies.
Braving the bandito Vasquez,[6]
With a little help from their friends Francisco and Manuela
Trujillo[7], her mother Jesusita Morales, their small sons
Dolores and Polito, and doomed daughter Aleja;[8]
Rancher Columbus Mose Cheney and wife Lucy Jane Stewart[9]
and their tiny Tom,
Mose's sister Lizzie and hubby George Harter
—dragged to death, hands holding his horses's reins—
Claude Morten Allen from Missouri, oak wood merchant,
German cabinetmaker August Schmidt and his crippled son,
Benjamin Frank and Mary Carroll Failor,
Beekeepers of fame, well-driller Joseph Robison,
Husband to Topanga teacher Ethel Berkey,
Joined by Joe's brother Will who married Mabel
And the Greenleafs with their orchards of apples and pears...

What did they do when the Moon rose over Topanga?
Mayhap they sat beneath live oaks, old even then,
Telling tales, quaffing some potent drink or not,
Debating politics, the future,
Grateful to sleep in paradise?

Her Majesty the Moon has seen it all
She keeps our tales, our lives, there in her secret hall
Where only the starry-eyed can see
Topanga holds her magic well
By The White Queen's will

1 Many thanks to *The Topanga Story* ed: Louise Armstrong York, published by The Topanga Historical Society.

2 Name for indigenous inhabitants, thus Topanga. Speaking 'Shoshonean', they were called the Gabrielino, people of the Mission San Gabriel in Central Los Angeles (never a name they called themselves). The Tongva died out before detailed historical records could be made. The boundaries with Chumash territory are at Malibu Creek.

3 From Sonora, Mexico, whose parents had emigrated from Spain.

4 Married at the Old Plaza Church in LA May 2, 1878.

5 Garrapata (Sp: sheep tick) is on early maps from the stream along the highway from Summit Valley to the confluence with Topanga Creek near the present post office. Garapito (Sp: small insect, tick) is given on U.S.G.S. maps to the creek through Sylvia Park along Cheney Drive. Early settlers in Old Canyon called their location "Topanga" (from the creek) or sometimes "Calabasas" whilst settlers in the 'new' canyon called it "Garapatos". The new Post Office (1908) chose the name "Topanga".

6 Not wanting settlers in the canyon, Vasquez challenged Santa Maria but when he found it was the former mail rider, he backed down. This must indicate the respect postmen were due in those days!

7 Also from Sonora, Mexico (1867), where the military actions of Emperor Maximilian drove many to seek freedom in the USA.

8 Born 1891, she moved to town in her early teens, married at 16 and died of TB at 25.

9 Arrived in "Garapatos Canyon" March 28, 1891.

Neighbors Kurt and Lisa

The Day Edison Turned Off The Lights[1]
For Sparky and Jill

The day Edison[2] turned off the lights,
Falling deeper into the Upanishads[3],
Walking out with saints and yogis, desert wanderers,
I chanced upon a woman raised in Kentucky whose pacifist brother
Moved to Costa Rica to avoid living in a country dealing in
                                                                weapons.

Atop the Santa Monica Mountains,
I meditated upon the matter of light.
Getting off the grid liberating me
                              from our online consuming culture.
Back on tv tells tales a-wanting, tomorrow clothes want washing,
dishwasher demanding, Powerbook writing, microwave messing,
roaster toasting, mind miscoping[4].

But before Edison ever turned on the lights,
AC/DC Wars pit futuristic scientist Tesla[5]
                                        against capitalist opportunist;
Industrial chicanery held at bay by utopian genius.
Together they harnessed Niagara and lit up New York City.
Actually, clearly,
We're always on a great grid, destined, confined.
Meantime, cacti prickle, squirrels steal,
                              blue jays squawk, peacocks preen,
Here, high up in Topanga,
Close to heaven, happy as the day is bright.

1 Written October 3, 1996. In 2001, an artificially greed-induced California
  electricity crisis became a real problem.
2 Thomas Edison (1847-1931).
3 Ancient, esoteric religious Hindu texts.
4 Poetic license and new word making, the poet's gift ...
5 Nikola Tesla (1856-1943): Croatian-born inventor of alternating current and a
  system for broadcasting free power worldwide. The AC/DC War was a power
  struggle for electricity-dominance between Tesla (eventually in league with
  George Westinghouse) and Edison. See *Prodigal Genius* by John J. O'Neill.

Out of Time

For Richard in retrospect, concerning the end of our ten year marriage, on the eve of our would-be wedding anniversary

How to walk out of time
In tune
    To hear the music of the spheres
Once again
    To face the alphabet of my desire[1]
With the gods

Today
    The sun shines heady through a hard Topanga sky
    Tawny hawks wheel, black ravens glide by
    The Old Ones remind me how I came and why
    My consort fell
          into a time-spelt fantasy of his own words.[2]
Tonight
    The White Queen watches
          from the corner of a golden eye
    As I pack black bags in haste
          against the falling of this moon
    My Cherokee drum safe,
          Navajo rattle, Chumash clacker at hand
    For the journey back across Turtle Island
Tomorrow
    I will unweave a tapestry of spent desires
    Semen gone astray in an ocean of tossing letters
    A long way gone from grunt and sign
    A cave of memories awaits the timeless soul
Out of time

1 Written under the influence of Leonard Schlain's *The Alphabet Versus the Goddess: The Conflict Between Word and Image* (1998) about the Goddess versus Patriarchy (her vs history).
2 Richard, deep into writing *Return to Ciuatlan*, was developing his anima female character Kelli. Time is a serious theme in that work, as in his major opus *Shades of Time*.

Between Trees
For Barbara S.

Today
I finally lay
In the hammock,
Between two trees
Letting everything else go
I watched the silver planes pass by
And white oleander blossoms drop gently down
The green of leaves the blue of sky the black birds

It was everything I could ask for, one of those peak
Moments the rest my life will filter through
Waiting for the next one until I
Gather enough to weave a
Tapestry of high desire
To present to
The White
Lady

Hall, Stairs and Landing

today we met at the Mimosa
the French café *a la* Topanga
where Brits regurgitate
lives unlivable at home
arriving with inedible dreams
waking up in a predictable America
emerging rich or poor, famous or not
what matters, a fantasy freedom
from confines of council houses
hall, stairs and landing up almost alive
childhood friends pushing prams
thickening unrecognizably on terrible food
still, missing their pubs
they aver the weather remains too good to be true

Life in the Canyon

Twice in seven days yellowjacket messengers[1]
Stop me stepping out to make a sinister wheel deal
Decisions detrimental leading to unknown disasters
Minding their own business but mending mine
Meantime
Down at the trading post
Where Tongva and Chumash bartered and shamans held court
Sacred and secular[2] clash, outcome easy to forecast
In a culture where good business means growth and development
Meanwhile
Dust mingles with scent of pine
Graceful pepper trees sweep blue skies, lacy leaves stir in the breeze
We bathe in shadows through long hot days
Sun baking gold ground, grass, tree and bush
                    await marine morning dew to drink again.

1 'Yellowjackets': a species of wasp.
2 A recent Topanga development dispute that centered on the Pine Tree Circle
  site downtown.

*Members of the "Brotherhood of Sound" mixing the bands at Topanga Days, our
Labor Day weekend extravaganza. L to R: Richard, Tomlinson Holman, Al Zang.
Photo probably by Mark Gander.*

The Brotherhood of Sound
For Dennis Fink, Mark Gander, Nigel Shaw, & Jerry del Colliano

Cronos,[1] god before the gods,
Before that suffering god upon a cross,
Decreed a mystery to unfold

By digital or analogue device
Live sound or artifice
By magicians modern or old as yet untold

To count the measure
Of our sway from Harmonia Mundi[2]
Accorded to originating sin

How many beats and stops
Flats and sharps
Would return divine *Alleluia* once again?

Now, what say our sound sages of golden ears[3]
In these days of music-mad devotees
To gross variations on the Music of the Spheres?

Will this Brotherhood
Unspell us from a grey cacophonous cone[4]
Unto *Allegro con Spirito,*[5] a brighter tone?

Lead us into an audio revolution[6]
The like of which we have not heard
Since Pythagoras played descant to the pipes of Pan?

1 God or Titan, embodiment/metaphor of/for Time
2 *Harmonia Mundi*, a classical record label BUT really, a magical esoteric term
  for The Harmony of the World as related to The Music of the Spheres. In
  French, *Le Chant du Monde.*
3 Like Bob Ludwig, one of the USA's leading mastering engineers.
4 Allusion to the cone of power raised by witches and mages.
5 Musical term: 'Lively with Spirit.'
6 See Jerry del Colliano's website: *www.audiorevolution.com*

With Sandi In Malibu

Sandi hails from South Africa
Where a new order
Is being born out of apartheid

She sings of African earth
Happy to be called home
To her perplexed paradise

We walk alongside
A car-infested beach
Sun and sand filtering through
We speak of this and that
A cadence
Of sadness and joy

Problems
Here there past present beset
This princess too regal to wait

In the big jungle dine-out
Of Greater LA
She has a greater role to play

Meantime she hangs out in Topanga
Where seasons of green and gold
Nourish the soul

Mother Africa
Shines within this golden girl
Waiting to tell an Old World A New Tale

Lady of the Beasts
For Toni and Tana

Here in Topanga, Canyon of the old gods
Your devotees hover and swarm
Big Bird of Isis[1] on border patrol,
His ladies in-waiting falling in behind
Master Blue Jay cawing,
Confronting Caitlín, a would-be Celtic Bast of a Cat
Lady Bug blessed with sad tales,
Legions of Ants marching all in Roman rows
Queen Arachne's at home here, Sir Cricket too,
But Little Snakes hide away
Whilst high in the sky Hawks and Eagles rule the day,
At night Owls come out to play
And Coyotes and Dogs at each other do bay

You live at the heart of the matter,
      in this tangible mystery school
Where we sit at the foot of masters,
      our Mistress marking essays in fight or flight
Be-spelling us for future enchantments

1 Peacocks

The Black Liberty Lady in Pink
For Betty B.

This was so good I have to tell it straight.
We went to a charity concert featuring Jackson Browne
It seemed ages we sat around round tables clustered
With little or no possibilities for forward movement
When finally after a peculiar Mexican meal
The action commenced
And it got interesting but the best part of the night
Apart from a tap dancing bonanza featuring one middle-aged
      three young blacks and one Hispanic hunk
Was the poem about the statue of liberty by a black gal in a
      tight-fitting up the crotch slippery shiny pink dress
She wrote it when she was twenty-one

She asked all the women to stand (no mention of color, that would
have been politically incorrect with that audience)
To hold their tight-fisted right arms in the air
To rounds of nervous laughter
We all did
We were with her all the way through her stunning diatribe
Against injustice to black women in America through the centuries
It was good to feel what she felt, see what she saw, know
we may overcome.

Salvation Shall Come From The South
For all unappreciated Good Men from the South

Marvin and Maynard, Mexican super Sears men
Made my December day, delivering
A pristine fridge, fashioning
A fruit-picker from plastic pipe and hanger
Together we tumbled the golden balls[1]
Whilst the sun shone high in the sky

The Goddess Calafia must have sent them by

The guys who installed air-conditioning
Against the heat of June, July and August.
The chap who roto-rooted the drains
In sweet September's bliss.
The man who cleaned the eaves
Of October November's leaves.

Her fix-it fellows everywhere you find

An overwhelming willingness to serve.
A gratefulness feigned or not, keeping
Deeper counsel from the gringo's grasp
An industriousness of immeasurable value.
Little wonder illegal immigrants are welcomed
Here in the Land of Milk and Honey:

The human engine that runs the golden state
The guardians, the keepers of us all, with
Their mellow dark and mindfulness of fate.
Never underestimate their meaning
Or their grace, for as we caught the
Grapefruit in their fall Marvin reminded me

He too read poetry before his Fall into the American Dream

1 Grapefruit on the tree in the yard

The Atlantis Trip
For my friend Beth Hapgood, on having just read
Colin Wilson and Rand Flem-Ath's Blueprint for Atlantis

This headlong quest for the true-story
100,000 years and mounting
Mesmerizing me.
Thank goodness they're doing the footwork.
I feel I want to slap them on the back.
Keep up the good works, boys!
I'll even bring the tea and bikkies to the battleground.

Where in gods' name[1] are they taking us?
– Now it's Antarctica –
But I'm with you guys
If it's gotta be there that paradise was
Let's do something extraordinary about those ice sheets
Covering up the evidence.
I'm not kidding, I'm keen to be on board.

Over the years I've read most of the books
Out there on this whole matter
I'm glad Rand has said the axis is getting less steep and we're *safer*
That we have over *29000* years till the next mantle displacement

Nonetheless I want it solved in my lifetime
I want those right wing Christian fundamentalist creationists to
                                                        eat fossils
Those diehard fixed Egyptologists and stuck geologists and
                                            unimaginative academics
To give up the ghost
To say, after all, we are older than we thought
And our worldview is pretty slim
But most of all, I want to be prepared with other earthlings
For the next one hundred thousand years like our incredibly
                                                wise ancestors were
We need to think ahead, not to speak of the miserable mess
We're in environmentally.

So yes, Atlantis is a worthy subject of debate
After all, not just for air heads and hippies.
What are we afraid of after all?
To know we aren't as advanced as we pretend to be?
Knowing the true story will surely make us work together
For the betterment of all, take us out of tribal chaos
Into the glorious Age of Aquarius
                                the gods told us would come

1 Elohim suits probably.

Goddess gathering at Chalice Well, Glastonbury (Photo: Cheri Barstow)

Cowgirl Tale:
Another One for Brigit[1]
For Jan B.

Canyon spirits tell long-tall tales
in split-level granite, live oak and coyote call
The spirits of Chumash and Tongva linger still
mythic realities meet and cross
Buffalo Calf Woman beckons
as Europa,[2] beloved white cow from the East,
Holy Hathor come again,
wanders across the wild West
over a wide prairie sea
chewing fragments of Aryan[3] epics
whose enigmatic meaning unravels
Ulysses' ongoing Iliad, Penelope waiting
weaving a tapestry of high desire
an old goddess enshrined in a dark cupboard
she secretly opens by night to feed and consult
Hera's due, ancient Isis,
White Lady of enlightened lands
washed by waters thick with black gold, seeds of life,
we are Her cowgirls, milk maidens all in a row
telling tales by hearth and fireside
the blood venerable in our veins
running in rivers to dark seas, mirrors of memory
we are, we are not, all that we can be

---

1 Brigit/Bride, goddess of wells and fire, to whom 'Brideswell' is dedicated, is
  linked with Hathor, Egyptian cow-goddess, great Goddess Isis, nourisher of
  nomadic cow-herding tribes. In Christianity she becomes St Bridget/Brigit,
  Bride, nanny to Jesus!
2 Europa, mythic metaphor for Europe, imaged as a sacred White Cow with
  whom Zeus, king of gods, mates, producing 'western civilization,' the effect of
  eastern Greek culture on the 'western world'.
3 In the original, non-Nazi sense, referring to ancestors from the east, the conjec-
  tured Indo-Europeans/Iranians, from Sanskrit *arya*, "noble."

On the Deck With Florence
For my daughter Kim-Ellen (pictured)

On the deck we sit and muse, mother's life passes by
An elegant old clipper with linen white sails
Her ship's log complete with the most minute details
Mixed with philosophical considerations
Portholes, escape hatches through which we wriggle
Mermaids tossed in gulf streams and oceans infinite

My Nova Scotia childhood comes alive
The gray Atlantic roar, those too real bedtime stories
Since Treasure Island lay right offshore,
Magnet to any kid worth their salt
Bent on buried treasure, brother Ralph and I
Built a sturdy pontoon raft and sailed her hence
Only to be saved by serious men in yellow slickers

Storied waves of memories
Sheets of sunlight blowing in a maritime wind
Passing through, remarking making me
Gathered in gene encoded bubbles
Deep down inside my daughter's well
Whose waters of life still await another
Passing

PS: Mom says that women who wore white
boots in wartime were floozies of the first order

Footnotes for the poem opposite:

1 Helen Koppejan: of Dutch Huguenot origins, born a Leo, a spiritual grand-mother of Glastonbury, without whose help the Isle of Avalon Trust and linked projects would not, at the very least, prospered. Teacher and author: *The Zodiac Image Handbook* (Element Books 1990)
2 Anciently known as a bird dedicated to Isis: see below
3 Of Egyptian origins 'Queen-Goddess' Isis sought Osiris, husband-lover-king, betrayed/confined in a custom-built coffin by his brother Set, murdered/pieces of his body dispersed/ finding only his penis, reconstructed, conceives and births her son Horus who revenges him. My Osiris: my then ex-husband, later re-found.

Wisdom of the Cave
On Processing the Aftermath of Divorce
For Helene Koppejan, in gratitude and remembrance

Helene,[1] lioness astrologer to Avalon,
        named my trials the twelfth labor of Hercules:

The hero battles the lion in the cave
Away from the public eye
His hidden battle makes him human
He steps over the threshold of mere accolade
Purpose purified, his soul awakes, spirit soars,
High deeds thenceforth to be trusted

In this canyon-cave retreat replete with scorpion, spider, rattler
        and royal peacock,[2]
And other unfamiliar shapes of timeless elementals
        catching private eyes
Re-awakening to living mythology, like Isis,
        hunting down her hero husband[3]
Finding his generative organ, conceiving golden Horus,
        Time by any other name,
I too sought his remains, something to re-member him by
        as she did of old
Searching his place of passion, retrieving it from coffin-tree
        wherein the dark one buried it
Thus do all women for love of man take this journey
        in image of Isis

What battles yet to come? Who is the lion in and of my soul?
Why, I do play all roles, betrayed, betrayer, goddess queen
        deliverer and devourer.
Hercules faced the lion in his soul. The lioness faces Hercules,
        hero of her soul.
Pride. Humility. Service. Sacrifice. Anima. Animus.

We all surrender.
Lady in White, guide us well.

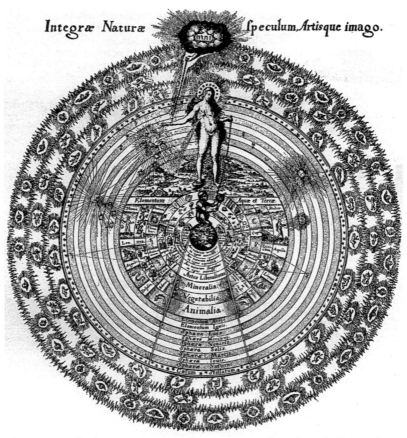

This engraving by de Bry appears in Collectio Operum *by Robert Fludd (1574–1637), and illustrates the latter's Rosicrucian principles. Above the three fiery rings of the Empyreum wherein dwell celestial creatures, is the sacred name of Jehovah encircled by clouds, from which issues a hand holding a chain linked to the arm of the woman, who perhaps represents the Universe. Her other hand holds a chain linking her to the ape-man on the terrestrial globe, which is surrounded in turn by human studies; mineral, vegetable and animal spheres; the four elements; and the planets and fixed stars.*

Divine Space

Make place
For divine space
For magic mystery mythic meaningful
Depth and perspective
Otherwise, unwise, the people perish…

AFTERWORDS

The One Work

*In remembrance of Captain and Aileen Ross-Stewart,
Sir George Trevelyan, Peter Caddy[1]
and That Committed Esoteric Great Generation*

*The One Work – what we embody on planet earth to accomplish –
through the physical, emotional, mental and intellectual into more
spiritual levels, from lower 'astral' to higher 'abstract' and beyond.[2]*

We are all born with an internal blueprint–stored in that inner
space humankind once did not to hesitate to name 'soul,' the rein-
carnated entity that accumulates experience. Soul incarnates with
the body and separates from it at death. Abiding on inner planes,
it continues learning, until, in conjunction with other aspects of
the Higher Self (versus the small self embodied in successive per-
sonalities), including soul guides and teachers, it reincarnates
again. Until an amazingly long and difficult journey is accom-
plished, whereby the soul moves onto another plane of being.
Several traditions envision this process of reincarnation in league
with all other souls and entities, this One Work. It is of utmost
importance to become aware that The One Work involves all
souls, inspirited entities, and in addition, mineral, plant and ani-
mal, as well as invisible but nonetheless real, angelic, elemental
and nature spirit realms (whatever a culture names them). In this
way of seeing *all that is*, over countless eons, 'we' (living souls or
sparks in human bodies) pass through and are part of all levels,
animate and non-animate.

In the process of a lifetime, even the most skeptical human may
catch a glimpse of this cosmic web, encompassing not only earth
but also our solar system and beyond: The Whole. Every child
looks up to the starry sky, asking similar questions: *who am I,
where am I and why am I?* We who parent and/or teach answer
from the limitations of our understanding. With conditioning, we
accept mundane cultural answers. To live and die well, if not
exceptionally, being of use to The Whole, is often viewed in the
confines of a religious rather than a broader spiritual context.
Religion provides useful leads. Then, as individuals, with a little

help from our friends on outer and inner planes, we hopefully grow our soul. But we all participate in The One Work. For those embracing the modern scientific world vision, explanations are steeped in language of matter, from the physics of very large to very small. For religiously-minded, parables and 'good books' backed up by good works provide legitimacy. For atheist and agnostic, *IT* is an acceptable Unknown, whilst for Buddhists, it is an illusion to be seen through (another level of mystery). For the magician and the mystic (two sides of a coin), ritual, ancient wisdoms, mythology and intuition exude the origins of All That Is, The Greater Mysteries.

In the process of wakening to The One Work, many leave one field of endeavour, successful or not, for one more connected (in the individual mind) with service to humanity or the planet, often in fields of healing, counseling and various forms of charity. In times past more entered priesthoods, monasteries and nunneries, just as pilgrimages were more obviously journeys for sacrifice than holidays with a difference. The urge to make one's life meaningful and service-orientated is universal. If this occurs in early adulthood it may be due to being born with good karma and/or genetic disposition. It may take till mid-life or old age to surface seriously. Fulfilling the need to live meaningfully, beyond the urge to leave descendents or simply a good name. For those who do not, cannot or refuse to 'awaken' there is always 'next time.' They may live with deep frustration, never finding 'purpose in life.'

It isn't just about obvious good works in charitable foundations; it's about one's chosen or destined role in The One Work, finding one's place. Teaching in a crowded inner city school, serving as an ethical merchant or service within family. And finally, The One Work involves inner growth, service to the soul itself, helping it grow up, thus serving the 'group soul' of humanity and its greater purpose in the Great Plan.

1 Ross, beloved former Head of Findhorn's Board of Trustees, and his equally beloved wife Aileen who carried on The One Work after his death: members of the 'Great Generation' including such old friends as Sir George Trevelyan and Findhorn's co-founder, Peter Caddy.
2 One fine fiction portrayer of the One Work in contemporary times is Doris Lessing in the *Shikasta* series: characters wakening to their genetic-encoded life purposes.

About the Author
Leona Graham-Elen BA Hons., MA (Canada)

After exchanging a Canadian academic career for the adventures of the 'alternative' movement in the 70's, Leona joined the spiritual and ecological Findhorn Community in NE Scotland. By the late 80's she had also taken an active role in that other great British community, Glastonbury—Ancient Avalon—helping found and run various educational organizations, as well as running for the Greens in 1992's General Election. In 1994 she and her partner Richard Elen moved to Bell Buckle, Tennessee, and in 1996 to Topanga, California. Whilst serving as Program Director with the International Center for Earth Concerns, the WILD Foundation, and the Cheetah Conservation Fund (USA) in Ojai, California, she always kept close working ties with Findhorn and Avalon.

*Nephew and niece
Alex and Lara Graham.
"...may the One Work
continue through our children..."*

My Family and Friends: Thank You!

If space permitted, biographies of all my cherished family and friends would appear here, not only the ones who have so generously contributed to this work—to whom I extend deep gratitude—but all of you who constitute the fabric of my incredibly rich 'social' life. Including your contributions reveals in a small way how important you are to me, and indicates what our human community is capable of: deep personal links that may last a lifetime, and perchance, forever. I hope that in our local and global communities we will find a way forward to making living on Earth a finer and better experience for all of us, that our children and their children down the ages will know that we, their ancestors, were part of the solution in learning how to share Earth life more equably with all her creatures and realms of existence in the Spirit of Friendship.

—*Leona*